THE WORLD'S **TOUGHEST**
ENDURANCE CHALLENGES

Note

While every effort has been made to ensure that the content of this book is as technically accurate and as sound as possible, neither the authors nor the publishers can accept responsibility for any injury or loss sustained as a result of the use of this material.

Published by Bloomsbury Publishing Plc
50 Bedford Square
London WC1B 3DP
www.bloomsbury.com

First edition 2012, reprinted 2013

ISBN 978 1 4081 5885 2

Acknowledgements

Cover photography: front © www.racingtheplanet.com (top), www.extremeworldraces.com (bottom); back © Gary Perkin/Cape Epic.
Inside photographs: see page 208
Illustrations by David Gardner
Designed by Austin Taylor
Commissioned by Charlotte Croft
Edited by Nick Ascroft

Ironman, Red Bull, Garmin, Craft-Nova, INOV-8, Subway, Hilton, Coke, Volvo, Specialized and Thule are all registered trademarks.

This book is produced using paper that is made from wood grown in managed, sustainable forests. It is natural, renewable and recyclable. The logging and manufacturing processes conform to the environmental regulations of the country of origin.

Typeset in 10.25pt on 13.75 Scala Sans Light

Printed in China by C&C Offset Printing co., Ltd.

This book is dedicated to all those people who take on life's challenges. Who don't accept the everyday. Who push themselves to their physical and mental limits. And who set out in the attempt to achieve something amazing.

THE WORLD'S **TOUGHEST** ENDURANCE CHALLENGES

RICHARD **HOAD** AND PAUL **MOORE**

Contents

Introduction

People have to learn sometimes not only how much the heart but how much the head can bear.

Maria Mitchell

tough

Adjective, adverb, noun, verb. Definition:

1 capable of great endurance; sturdy; hardy
2 difficult to perform, accomplish or deal with
3 vigorous; severe; violent

At this very moment, somewhere in the world people are pushing themselves to the very limit of human endurance. Whether they are in a desert, up a mountain or under the sea, they have reached the physical and mental 'edge'. They are exhausted, doing their best to simply survive. Not everyone does. But a lot – most, in fact – live to tell the tale. The tale of a challenge that they faced up to and ultimately overcame. The tale of the pain, the exhaustion and, finally, the exhilaration of achieving something that will not only define them as an individual but also help them to realise goals that are, for many people, inconceivable.

Humans have been doing this since the birth of recorded time. From explorers like Marco Polo and Ibn Battuta, who willingly set off into the distance determined to discover whatever it was that lay beyond the horizon, to the trailblazers of the eighteenth and nineteenth centuries, whose explorations provide the routes for some of the challenges that feature in the pages of this book, we have constantly pushed ourselves to go further and faster than ever before.

Why do they – actually, why do we – do it? That's an impossible question to answer. But many of the people who take part in these events, who attempt to complete these challenges, do share one common motivation. In the early 1920s George Mallory was asked why he wanted to climb Mount Everest (at that point considered to be the toughest endurance challenge on the planet). In three simple words he summed up the motivation of so many who both preceded and followed him: 'Because it's there.'

These three words are the driving force behind a very small, very select group of people. A group of latter-day adventurers and athletes who are not content simply completing – and competing – in what is deemed to be the norm. A group of individuals who want to see how much their bodies and minds can tolerate before they reach breaking point. And a group of people who will tackle a challenge that 99.99% of the human population would consider crazy. They do it because it is there.

But this book isn't about personal motivation. There are no tips on kayaking one of the toughest water systems in the world or techniques on surviving your umpteenth day in the open, without sleep, while trying to reach a nigh-on unobtainable goal. Instead, it is a celebration of these challenges.

We have chosen 50. Of course, there are more. Around the globe, ultra-endurance challenges are becoming increasingly popular. In fact, many of the challenges that were once considered tough are now considered a little passé. Ironman? Try the Arch to Arc. Marathon? Heard of the legendary Western States 100?

People all over the world are pushing themselves harder and further than ever before. What's more, they seem to enjoy doing it in some of the most inhospitable conditions Mother Nature can throw at them.

So how have we chosen the challenges that will appear in this book? First off, let us just say that it hasn't been easy (but it has been fun). There are hundreds – fast becoming thousands – of ultra-distance challenges out there. A small number of them are known throughout the world, a large number of them are known by only a handful of people. And there are many races or challenges that you will undoubtedly have heard of but which do not appear in these pages. Climbing Mount Everest is one, cycling around the world another. And there is a reason for that.

When we started compiling this list of challenges, we quickly realised that we had to lay down some guidelines, otherwise pretty much anything could feature. So, after much soul-searching and careful consideration, we came up with the following stipulations.

Each challenge must:
- Have an organising body that outlines rules and restrictions on participation.
- Be open to public participation (i.e. it is not a professional race).
- Have a pre-determined start and end point.
- Have a way of categorising participants based on finish times/positions/achievement.
- Be really, really tough.

Hopefully, from these guidelines, you can see why cycling/walking/pogo sticking the world or climbing Mount Everest does not fit the bill. Nor, for that matter, does a race like the Tour de France – a supreme test of human endurance.

Similarly, some of the challenges in the book are definitely achievable – most, in fact (with varying demands on your dedication). But laying down guidelines was an integral part of this project – and one that allowed us to determine what are the toughest endurance challenges on the planet.

Of course, with so many races of varying sizes in existence, there is a (remote) chance that we have overlooked something or missed out a true beast. We don't think that we have. But if we have and you are an organiser or participant of the race, get in touch. We'll twist the arm of our publisher to give us a second bash and you'll be in (as long as you meet the criteria). In the meantime, sit back, relax and enjoy this anthology of the 50 toughest endurance challenges on the planet.

Not only are they a testament to what people can achieve, they will hopefully provide you with the inspiration you need to tackle something truly formidable.

Go on, you know you want to ...

How Tough?

The challenges that competitors in these races face are numerous. In fact, it would be impossible to list them all. However, to help facilitate an understanding of some of the major obstacles athletes face, we have tried to group them into 10 key areas:

Cold

out of water Prolonged periods of exercise in cold weather can reduce peak oxygen uptake (VO_2 max) and cardiovascular performance. When muscles cool beneath a certain temperature (27°C/82°F), the ability to perform for an extended period of time decreases. Dehydration is a significant consideration, with athletes less inclined to drink but the body still requiring regular hydration. If body temperature falls below 35°C (95°F), hypothermia sets in and in extreme cases this can be fatal.

in water When the body loses heat due to constant exposure to cold, the blood flows to the vital organs (to keep them functioning). The blood flows away from the arms and legs, making the swimmer feel weaker. Prolonged exposure to cold water can lead to hypothermia – a dangerous cooling of the core body temperature – which can in extreme cases be fatal.

Altitude

Prolonged periods of exercise at altitude (for those not accustomed to it) can have a profound impact on athletic performance. Above 1500m (4900 feet) the lack of oxygen can lead to an increased breathing rate, higher heart rate, nausea, headaches and sleeplessness. What's more, at higher altitudes athletes' VO_2 max decreases and so performance is impacted. In extreme cases altitude sickness can be fatal.

Heat

The impact of an increase in body temperature (hyperthermia) on the human body reduces the efficiency of the muscles, reduces the ability of the heart to move the blood around the body, and moves the metabolism from primarily aerobic to anaerobic (placing a strain on the carbohydrate stores in the body). In addition, athletes need to manage their hydration, as the body loses more fluid during prolonged periods of exercise at higher temperatures.

Distance

All but a very small number of the races featured in the book take place over exceptional distances. But a few ask competitors to cover an extraordinary distance. These distances are, of course, relative to the sport. However, the sheer ground needed to be covered – and the time taken to do so – can have an incredible impact on the performance and psychology of the athlete.

Mental

As with distance, all the challenges featured in this book require exceptional mental strength. However, there are a few that require athletes to be in complete control of their minds to deal with factors ranging from absolute solitude to utter relaxation and even mind-numbing boredom. Mastering the mind against these factors is essential to successfully completing the challenge.

Elevation change

Extreme ascents or descents place considerable strain on an athlete's body. Physically, the greatest challenge in running or cycling uphill is fatigue. The impact of ascending in these sports should not have the same risk as descending, though. This will place strain on runners legs (the 'anti-gravity' muscles stretching while trying to contract) and increase the potential to fall and get injured, especially when legs are fatigued. Descending on any kind of bike is a technical skill and can markedly impact race outcomes.

Technical

The technicality of a particular challenge obviously varies with the demands of the sport itself. For instance, mountain bike ascents and descents can be incredibly technical, as can the ability to master a yacht or kayak in turbulent waters. As such, any challenge that cites technical as an issue requires solid – if not advanced – ability in the discipline. This technical ability can be even more important when environmental conditions become a factor.

Weather

The weather affects every race, but in some the extremes of weather and their potential impact on an athlete and their performance can be severe. If the weather is extremely hot, cold or simply changeable, athletes have to be able to adapt to their surrounds to stand a chance of getting to the finish line. As a variable not in competitors' control, even careful planning and kit preparation may not be sufficient to combat a potentially race-changing element.

Currents

Cited mainly for swim events in this book (although applicable to other events), the movement of tides and currents can have a significant impact on both the time and ability of an athlete to complete a challenge. All races affected by currents have to be carefully planned to give the athlete the optimum chance to complete, although when this is not possible or plans are not met, competitors are forced to deal with this uncontrollable force.

Terrain

Terrain can present major challenges for athletes, regardless of whether it is constant or variable. Snow, ice, sand, swamps, rivers or rock-strewn trails require extra physical strength to overcome. In environments where there are extremes of temperatures or conditions, any shifting, difficult terrain places a strain on athletes which can easily lead to injury. Changeable terrain can also cause athletes problems, sometimes requiring a change in technique and causing additional strain on often fatigued muscles.

EUROPE

Type Multi-discipline
Date August
Distance 226km (140 miles)
Main obstacles Elevation change
Website www.nxtri.com
They call it The world's toughest long-distance triathlon.

Competitors say
❛ *We signed up for a hardcore race, and they were delivering one right from the beginning.* ❜

Norseman

A breathless leap into the swirling, icy waters of a Norwegian fjord, a bike that climbs high into the mountains and a run that ends on the summit of a rocky peak combine to make one of the toughest single day sports events just that little bit harder.

below The most fabled swim in triathlon

There was a time when triathlon was very much a minority sport. In fact, most people didn't really know what it was. And Ironman? That was a mythical pursuit that only a few brave (and slightly foolish) souls attempted. Those days are long gone now, and the triathlon brand is energetically spreading its reach around the world. Expect loud music, thousands of spectators and feed points every few kilometres.

But there are still races – admittedly few and far between – that offer none of these perks. Instead, they continue to extol the core concept of long-distance triathlon: stoic determination. The Norseman is one of those. A 4km (2-mile) swim through the icy waters of a Norwegian fjord is followed by a 180km (112-mile) mountainous bike and finished off with a 42km (26-mile) run that takes competitors to the top of Gaustatoppen (1880m/6200ft above sea level).

It is a small race – 240 competitors board the ferry out into the Eidfjord at 4 a.m. in the morning – and it is basic. Competitors have to provide their own support crew who follow them throughout the race (and one of whom has to accompany the athlete up the final mountain climb), and at the finish line there's little to greet you except a lift that takes you back down through the mountain to your support car and team.

But that, perhaps, is the attraction of this race – the lack of glitz and glamour. Instead it is raw. Raw from start to finish.

Only those competing in the race are allowed to board the ferry that leaves at 4 a.m. From there it is the best part of an hour out to the start line 4km (2 miles) from the shore. The water is cold, it is deep, and to get to the start you have to jump off the back of the boat. From there things should, on paper, be pretty simple. And for those who are fast, strong swimmers it is (if they can navigate effectively through the early morning gloom). But the currents through the fjord can either help or hinder, and a tough 4km (2-mile) swim can become far harder when swimming against the flow of a draining fjord.

Out on the bike things don't get any easier: 1250m (4100 feet) of climbing greet the cyclists in the first 40km (25 miles),

left If the course doesn't get you, the weather will!

above The road is long ... but rewarding

and from there the notorious Hardanger plateau frequently sees the temperature drop and gusting winds sweep the barren vista. Needless to say, it isn't long before the climbing starts again, and competitors 'enjoy' numerous steep ascents and descents through some stunning Norwegian countryside.

Then there is the run. For many, the thought of tackling a marathon after 180km (112 miles) on a bike is tough enough. But to tackle one that is largely uphill … madness. Admittedly, the first 20km (12 miles) is relatively flat. Then, just as the legs are beginning to really hurt and the body has started to reject the nutrition it is being loaded up with, the hills begin in earnest. For the next 17km (10 miles), competitors climb. Only the first 160 are allowed to pass the 33km (20-mile) checkpoint and they have to do so within 14 hours, 30 minutes. Following that first check, the second cut-off point is just 2km (1.2 miles) further on – at 15 hours, 30 minutes – and that is the entry to the mountain.

Following a medical check, athletes have to be supported by one member of their team on this final 5km (3 miles) over a rocky, uneven ascent of Gaustatoppen, the highest mountain in the Telemark area.

And at the top? If it isn't dark, athletes are treated to a spectacular view of the Norwegian countryside. If it is dark, there's a cafeteria offering warm drinks and a place to sit down. Then, when the legs stop throbbing and the mind clears just a little, there is the choice of catching the lift through the heart of the mountain or walking back down again. Like the race itself, there are no frills here – and that is what makes it so special.

Those who do complete the entire race receive a black Norseman T-shirt. Those who do not make the final cut-off to climb the mountain but finish the full distance receive a white version. But for all of the competitors, there is a real sense of having accomplished one of the toughest, most spectacular single day races on the planet.

opposite An incredible finish awaits those who make the cut off

Drew Marlar

In other Ironman races they have course buoys set up along the swim route to keep you in line, but that is not Norseman's style. Dump 260 competitors into the middle of a dark fjord and point them in the general direction. I loved the simplicity of all this and the faith that the race organisers put in the athletes. We signed up for a hardcore race and they were delivering one right from the beginning. Cold and challenging, the swim started as the rest of the race would continue.

The first 19km (12 miles) of the bike are flat and fast. But before I knew it I was at Eidfjord, and this is where the fun began. In between the climbs were some great downhills and straight sections that allowed me to spin my legs out and recover for the next big effort. This scenery was the most beautiful that I had ever seen. Think of cycling out of the Grand Canyon but it is covered in a thick blanket of evergreens, moss and beautiful whitewater rivers. I was so lucky to be there and I let it all surround me. I was truly in the moment and could not have been happier.

A quick change and bathroom break and I was off on the run. This is the part of the race that makes it famous. At Mile 12 you get the first glimpse of what lies ahead and it looks ridiculous. Gaustatoppen is a scary huge mountain that is topped by a stark radio tower. This is a cruel and difficult finish to a marathon. The 'trail' is really just a bunch of loose rocks up steep ravines. You alternate climbing over huge boulders to slipping on loose scree. I hadn't really suffered yet today, but my time had come. Things were shutting down and I was focused on one thing – getting to that finish line and looking out at the valley below. The rocks got bigger and steeper and the way seemed so far still. Glancing back just made me dizzy and unbalanced. The last few steps were some of the toughest I've taken but I crossed that timing pad in 13 hours, 42 minutes and in 39th place.

I couldn't hold it in and I let my head fall back and tears ran down my cheeks. The whole point of these things is to prove how tough you are, but here I was at the finish and crying.

Drew Marlar completed the Norseman in 2011

Type Multi-discipline
Date July
Distance 880km (546 miles)
Main obstacles Weather, elevation change, technical
Website www.redbullxalps.com
They call it The world's most spectacular adventure race

Competitors say
❝This is much more than just an Alpine crossing; it's an adventure, an expedition and, at the same time, a competition.❞

The Red Bull X-Alps

From leaping off the top of the mountain to running through twisting, rugged valleys, the Red Bull X-Alps is a test of courage, speed, strength and resolve.

right Competitors must run over many miles of rough terrain

opposite top Mountaineering skills and experience in the mountains are a prerequisite

opposite bottom Flying is always the preferable – but not the safest – option

In 2003, Hannes Arch had the idea for an event that would take endurance racing to new heights. Arch wanted to see whether it was possible to traverse the length of the European Alps – from Salzburg in Austria to the Principality of Monaco – using just a paraglider and a pair of legs. It was an audacious project. Competitors would have to cover up to 546 miles (880km) in a short period of time, with limited assistance from a one-person support team.

However, in true Red Bull style, the audacious became reality and that year 17 athletes launched off the Dachstein Glacier en route to Monaco (via Zugspitze, Mont Blanc and Mont Gros). Kaspar Henny was the first of three men to complete the inaugural race, reaching the principality in just under 12 days. Despite the high dropout rate a legendary race was born.

A biennial event, the Red Bull X-Alps takes place on 'odd' calendar years. The field that starts the race is understandably small, and entry is hard to come by. The race organising committee select up to 30 competitors (with two wildcard entries available). Every athlete who takes part in the race has to hold an official paragliding licence and be an experienced mountaineer. Not to mention being exceptionally physically fit.

Athletes have been known to paraglide as little as 40 per cent of the course en route to finishing in Monaco. That can mean stretches of up to 80km (50 miles) continuous running (with paraglider strapped on their back) before climbing the next mountain and launching yet again. In fact, even the most skilled paragliders – who will spend as much as 75 per cent of their time in the air – need to be strong runners to

stand a chance of finishing within the 48-hour cut-off time following the winner's arrival in the principality.

But in truth, those who are able to master and manage their paraglider are most likely to be the ones that cross the line at the head of the field. The distances that they are able to cover – and thus the energy they are able to conserve – while passing through some of Europe's most spectacular scenery makes a huge difference. But it isn't easy. Conditions in the Alps can turn ugly very quickly, and all competitors must be adept at launching off the side of a mountain into headwinds sometimes beyond recommended paragliding limits, which takes supreme skill and courage. In these

conditions, competitors have been known to drop more than 1000m (3300 feet) in less than five minutes as their paragliders struggle to stay airborne in turbulent skies. At the same time, understanding the movement of the wind and thermals through mountain valleys takes an innate ability, and those who have it retain a significant advantage over those who don't.

But endurance and paragliding skills mean nothing without the ability to scale some of the most dangerous peaks in Europe. It is estimated that up to 100 people die every year on Mont Blanc – one of the turning points on the race. And because of the uncertainty of the conditions and the fickle nature of Alpine weather, competitors are not only at the mercy of the elements in the air, but on exposed mountain faces as well. Complete white-outs, vicious snowstorms and sudden drops in temperature are not uncommon, and everyone who takes part in the race – competitor and support team alike – needs to know how to survive when the mountains get angry. The uncertainty of the weather walks hand in hand with the uncertainty of the mountain ascents needing to be tackled. No competitors can be 100 per cent sure of where they are landing, and at some point they will have to climb their way out of Alpine valleys. As such, climbing and mountaineering skills are as necessary as paragliding ability.

What's more, the course never gets easier. The 2011 edition of the race saw athletes tackle an 864km (537-mile) route between Salzburg and Monaco. On the way, competitors had to pass eight 'turn points' (essentially checkpoints), frequently located on some of the most inhospitable terrain in Europe.

Needless to say, with a select entry policy and highly skilled pilots, the times that the athletes record are quick.

The record is a few hours short of 10 days, with most winners coming in around the 11- to 12-day mark.

With a combination of the harshest weather conditions, most treacherous terrain, and one of the most dangerous sports on the planet, the Red Bull X-Alps is truly a unique event that comfortably takes its place among the elite endurance challenges.

Steve Nash

I had been training for this event, in the hope that I would get selected, more than 12 months before the start date. However, once we (that's me and my supporter Richard Bungay) were in, we incrementally increased our training right up to the event. This was very much the physical side for me, with sessions of off-road running and cycling every day. More specific and targeted training included: running ultra-distance races in the United Kingdom with an 11kg (24lb) paraglider on my back; fast ascents in the mountains with even faster descents on the paraglider; and as much paragliding as I could possibly get in the less-than-perfect UK climate.

Simply having enough time to prepare was a big issue. Although my employers were incredibly supportive in the lead-up to the event, as was my wife, it was still really difficult to find enough time to train and prepare.

Another major part of the preparations was to acquire all of the necessary lightweight flying, hiking and mountaineering gear that would be required. To do this meant a huge campaign to get a personal sponsor on board with our team. The efforts were well rewarded with a number of major names joining us: Garmin, Craft, Nova, INOV-8 to name a few.

My supporter Richard was the key to keeping me going whilst racing by effectively splitting the incredibly long race into manageable chunks. We'd arrange to meet up after a certain time or distance or maybe even a different country. By doing this the interim goal was my focus, and meeting him for food and drink was the most important thing to me.

After a great start running up a mountain, I made a poor decision in the air, which put me on the ground much earlier than most of my competitors. This meant that I had to dig real deep to launch again and try to catch up. Most of this was done on foot – some 50km (30 miles) or so. The ability to look objectively at a mistake and move on is so valuable. This was enhanced by our team decision not to recriminate in the event of mistakes or errors, which proved a wise decision as we only moved forwards towards our goal.

After 12 days, the race for our team came to an unplanned and very abrupt end on the same day that the winner made it into Monaco. At this point a huge storm had blocked our route to the Matterhorn (one of the eight turn points in the race) and I was faced with a difficult decision to either walk back down the 1400m (4593 foot) mountain that I had spent hours walking up for a good flight or try to fly in less-than-OK conditions towards the storm. I decided to fly, but in doing so had overlooked the fact that I was very close to controlled airspace, which would get me a penalty if I flew into it. The stress of trying to keep moving towards the goal dropped my guard, allowing me to fly into the airspace by 8m (26 feet) – I was disqualified from the race.

This was never a scenario we had contemplated as I am clinical in my adherence to rules and Richard had been constantly making me aware of difficult areas. In the immediate few hours after being told we could no longer race, we were absolutely empty, without feeling and it was hard to rationalise what had happened; that was until a flood of texts from friends who had been watching the events live, now pointing out that the race could have ended in a much worse way with serious injury or worse!

On reflection now, we both agree this race is unfinished business!

Steve Nash competed in the 2011 Red Bull X-Alps.

Type Foot
Date October
Distance 4132km (2567 miles)
Main obstacles Distance, mental
Website www.transeurope-footrace.org
What it takes Getting up every morning at around 4.30 a.m. and running an average of 60km (38 miles) per day.

Competitors say
6 *When racing I just focused on each day at a time, never looking further than completing that day.* 9

Trans Europe Footrace

A relentless march across Europe, the Trans Europe Footrace stops for no one and tests the hearts, minds and bodies of those who tackle this truly epic challenge.

It is safe to say that all the challenges in this book test the physical and mental strength of the participants. Of course, the degrees to which these faculties are examined vary from event to event and individual to individual. But few can honestly be said to strip competitors back to basics, providing a daily test of physical and mental determination. The Trans Europe Footrace is one such event.

Starting in Skagen, Denmark, the race heads south through Germany, France and Spain before finishing in Gibraltar. During the course of the 4132km (2567 miles), the 50 or so runners can expect to average some 60km (38 miles) per day in conditions that are best described as 'basic'. What's more, every stage has a cut-off time based on an average speed of 6km/h (3.7mph). Any competitors failing to sustain

that pace risk losing their official spot within the competition, although exceptions are made in certain circumstances.

Of course, for a seasoned ultra-distance runner 60km (38 miles) is a relatively trifling affair. However, to do that day after day on variable terrain places enormous strain on the lower body of the competitors. There is also a huge element of cumulative fatigue involved in racing this kind of event: it simply does not stop. Every day, the race moves forward from village to town, town to city. Those who cannot keep up are simply excluded from the event. As such, there is little – if any – time for injuries along the route, and the mental stress of maintaining pace and participation is huge.

This is a mental stress that is, in part, exacerbated by the conditions en route. The organisers make no secret

below Those who enter must prepare for a mentally and physically exhausting race

below right The pace and the route is relentless

of the fact that the lodging and food along the way is basic at best. Athletes are expected to bring their own air mattresses and sleeping bags, and the usual choice of overnight accommodation is a school gymnasium. If that is unavailable, a tent is an alternative option. Showers are far from guaranteed, hot water a luxury and forget about ice baths. This is ultra-distance running in its rawest form.

All of these conditions add to the stress placed on the body when racing the Trans Europe. Feet and legs bear an enormous amount of the burden in a race like this, and the basic nature of the post-stage accommodation makes TLC something of a luxury. As such, those intending to race in the event need to be prepared to manage their own recovery, and do it in an environment that is not amenable to pampering.

Food and hydration are, of course, another key consideration during the race. Aid stations are available every 10–12km (6–8 miles) along the route, but the contents of them are far from guaranteed. The organisers are beholden to local shops and outlets, meaning that athletes will have to cope with various types of solids, liquids and gels. Many ultra-distance athletes are quite particular about the type of food they consume during a race. What's more, they prepare their bodies in such a way as to be able to consume and digest certain food types while exercising. The uncertainty of what is provided along the way can therefore have a massive impact on the competitors, and can directly affect their ability to complete the race. Third-party help is strictly forbidden under race rules, so any support team cannot be supplying competitors with nutrition and hydration en route. In the Trans Europe, everyone plays by the same rules.

above This is a no-frills, simply hard work event

And they also follow the same route, although not everyone finds that easy. Of course, organisers try to clearly define the route of the race. But athletes are running solo from point to point, and weary minds and bodies do occasionally miss the massive arrows that run alongside the roads and paths that carry the competitors. In these instances, it is the athletes' duty to retrace their steps onto the race course (although the organisers will help them if they get really lost).

Despite the quite considerable challenges posed by the race, the achievements of those who complete it are impressive to say the least. Peter Bartel was the 2009 champion, leading home the field of 45 runners in a mere 352 hours, 3 minutes and 25 seconds. In the women's race Furuyama Takako secured victory in an impressive 529 hours, 6 minutes and 5 seconds.

All in all, the Trans Europe footrace is a brutal test of human endurance. The distance alone – and cumulative fatigue associated with it – is test enough. But when the physical demands of the race are coupled with the transient and basic nature of the accommodation, the challenge becomes even greater. For those who succeed in mastering it, the reward is simple: they have become one of the few people to run the length of Europe, and in so doing join an elite group of some of the most mentally and physically tough ultra athletes in the world.

Andreas Falk and Trond Sjåvik

ATHLETE PERSPECTIVE

Andreas Falk: I trained with a focus on the Trans Europe Footrace for three years, running longer and longer races in preparation. The last long race before the start was La Transe Gaule, a 1150km (720-mile) stage race. I worked with a mental coach before (and after) the race. I also focused on the small things, such as kit and nutrition.

Trond Sjåvik: Physical preparation was running, of course. The Deutschlandlauf 2007 (1200km/750 miles in 17 days) and La Transe Gaule 2008 (1150km/720 miles in 18 days) were important parts of my preparations. These races were also good mental training. The last three-and-half months before the start of the Trans Europe, I ran every day.

AF: The biggest challenge in my mind leading up to the race was: Would I be able to stay away from my family for the 70 days? When racing, I just focused on each day at a time, never looking further than completing that day. It also helped that I ran the entire race with a friend of mine, Matthias, which helped a lot to keep me going. My biggest issue in the race was that I got injured halfway through it. This forced me to walk for six days, although no slower than 10 minutes per kilometre (1100 yards) to keep to a certain pace. I even had to walk for a full 80km (50 miles) one day.

TS: The first half of the race, I had no real problems. When I got an injury – a shin splint – I had to forget about the competition, and just focus on getting from one water station to the next. During such a long event, most runners will face injuries or other problems. When it happens, all you can do is to be patient, treat it as well as you can, and hopefully you will get better day by day.

AF: It was a strange feeling to finish the race. I had one single goal for over three years, and when I made it to the finish line I had a feeling of emptiness. But I am very satisfied with completing the race on reflection: not many people have done things like that and being able to run the race together with Matthias made it even more special.

TS: The last two weeks of the race, I was fed up with it all. I could not see the point of going to Nordkapp (where the race finished). Why not stop in the middle of Sweden? It was long enough. When I finally arrived at Nordkapp, I was just happy it was over. The first weeks after coming home, I felt empty. Having no initiative to do anything. Working, of course, but the rest of the days doing nothing. I don't think much about the tour, my mind is working on future races, but now and then my girlfriend, who was also running the race, and I look at photos from the tour. Many good memories. I am happy that I did it.

Trond Sjåvik came sixth in the 2009 Trans Europe Footrace and has previously completed the 1200km Deutschlandlauf and the 1150km Transe Gaule.
Andreas Falk spent three years building up to the 2009 Trans Europe Footrace, including running the Transe Gaule.

Type Foot	Date July

Distance 230km (143 miles)

Main obstacles Heat, terrain

Website www.alandalus-ut.com

They call it Demanding and technical with high temperatures (35–40°C/95–104°F), numerous long climbs and scenic trails.

Competitors say
❝I will keep the memories of Stage Two, running down the mountain, legs tired, in company of deer, under the scorching sun: magical!!❞

SPAIN

Loja
Granada

National Park

Malaga

Al Andalus Ultimate Trail Race

A beauty and a beast: 230km (143 miles) of racing over five days through some of the most beautiful countryside in Europe. Paradise? Not quite. Scorching temperatures, unforgiving ascents and uneven tracks make the Al Andalus a true ultra-running test.

below The road is long, hot and over challenging terrain

An unforgiving sun beats down on an exposed mountain face. A narrow track weaves up towards the summit of the mountain, sometimes even but frequently interrupted by rocks large and small. It's hot – approaching 40°C (104°F) – and you still have 20km (12.4 miles) to run. And that's just on this stage. The real meat of the race hasn't even begun yet and the pain from the blisters on your feet is unbearable. But the test, the challenge – that is why you are here.

Set amid some of the most stunning scenery Europe has to offer, the Al Andalus Ultimate Trail Race pits athletes against harsh terrain and unforgiving heat over five brutal days. Like many races in this book, the sheer length of the course is manageable for those familiar with ultra-distance events. It is the variables confronting athletes along the route that makes the Al Andalus so challenging.

Firstly, there is the heat. The average temperature in Andalucia during the daytime in the middle of July ranges from 30°C to 45°C (86–113°F). Exercising for even a short period of time in this heat places an immense strain on the human body. But factor in that the shortest stage of the Al Andalus – the first – comes in at 37km (23 miles), and you begin to get a feel for the physical strain this places on each and every competitor. The longest stage is 68km (43 miles). As such, the need to fuel and hydrate effectively becomes even more imperative than usual, and knowing when your body needs to take a break from both exercising and the sun becomes essential for your race survival.

What's more, the course demands that athletes remain alert and focused at all times. The amount of simple road and path running is limited during the Al Andalus, with much of the course crossing rugged and uneven terrain. This obviously necessitates a need to focus at all times, as a misplaced

foot could easily end in a twisted ankle. As such, anyone attempting the race should have plenty of off-road, multi-terrain experience.

This becomes even more relevant when you consider the undulating nature of the course. Unlike some of the ultra-distance races featured in this book, the Al Andalus has gained a reputation not just because of the vertical metres climbed but also because of those descended. In fact, the cumulative descent on each stage of the trail (an average of around 1000m/3300 feet) is greater than the cumulative ascent (an average of around 900m/2900 feet). This places an additional strain on the lower body that is already fatigued from the ongoing impact of the race.

Along the route, there is some support for athletes, and race organisers transport the athletes' kit between stages.

below The race is highly competitive but good-natured

right A minimum amount of equipment must be carried by every competitor during every stage

above The Al
Andalus attracts some
quality athletes

This means that although competitors must carry a number of obligatory items – including food and electrolyte drinks, a head cover, whistle and compass – the race remains a pure running challenge. At the end of each stage, athletes stay in local villages, allowing them to immerse themselves in Andalucian culture and interact with the multinational community of runners who take on the race. While the Al Andalus is very challenging, competitors also benefit from the stunning surroundings and the opportunity to reconnect with nature on a basic level.

As per most ultra-distance races, there is a time limit on each stage based on a minimum average speed of 6km/h (3.7 mph). If competitors do not reach the finish in time, they will not have their total result counted (but can continue if they wish). Needless to say, not everyone finishes the race, and in 2011 only 44 of the 65 starters made it to the end. To determine the quality of the field, you just have to look at the time difference between the first and last athlete home. The winner in 2011 completed all five stages in a little over 19 hours, with the last runner

Helen Taranowski

In preparation for the race, I ran high weekly mileage (1062km/660 miles during May and June) with an emphasis on long runs. Sometimes I would do long runs on three consecutive days to get used to being on my feet for a long time, day after day. As I come from a road-running background, I had to switch to doing a lot of training off-road and over hilly terrain.

In the last ten days before the event, I had four heat acclimatisation sessions where I was running in a temperature of 35–40°C (95–104°F). I thoroughly tested out the kit I was planning to wear during the event, and the food and drinks I was going to use. The physical training I did was also part of the mental preparations, but I also studied the course maps, descriptions and elevation profiles for each of the stages in detail so that I had some idea what I would be facing each day. For two months of my life, every bit of spare time was consumed with preparation in some way.

My biggest obstacle in preparation for the race was that I was unable to do any exercise at all during April, as I had a minor operation at the end of March. This meant that in May I had to build up my running from zero back to high mileage very quickly. I had only eight weeks to get myself fit to compete, so I was constantly walking a fine line between increasing my fitness and risking overtraining.

The major issue in the race was on Stage Four, the long day; I was feeling ill right from the start of the day. I had struggled to eat my breakfast and when I started running, I was feeling very low in energy. Shortly after Checkpoint Three I was sick, and after that I was feeling so ill that I couldn't manage to take on any more food and only small amounts of fluid. I used every technique I knew to distract myself from how I felt. When I look back now, I have no idea how I managed to get to the end of the stage! I guess the competitive spirit in me just took over. I was leading the race, I had won the previous three stages, and while my legs were still able to carry me forward I would keep going – pulling out just wasn't an option for me!

When I saw the finish line, I just felt so happy to have completed the event because until the moment you cross that line you can never be sure that you are going to make it. So there were plenty of tears of relief and happiness. At that point I started to fully take in what I had gone though and achieved over those five days. To actually have won the event was unbelievable, especially as I had such a short time to prepare. Now, when I look back, I feel a huge sense of achievement, not just from winning the event but also from all the training I did and from discovering that my body is tougher and capable of much more than I once thought.

Helen Taranowski won the 2011 Al Andalus. For more information about Helen, visit www.helentaranowski.com

home in 30 hours, 30 minutes. At both ends of the spectrum, these are impressive times.

As with many ultra-distance races, the Al Andalus is not just about beating others, but about pushing yourself beyond what you might think is physically possible. While fatigue, terrain and the heat act as the main challenges, the exposure to nature and a local culture steeped in tradition offer their own rewards. The sense of shared experience among a small field of athletes means that the race, though highly competitive, is run in a good-natured and supportive environment. These unique aspects define the Al Andalus: it's a tough endurance run, but more than that it's a life-enhancing experience.

above Every step has to be considered

Type Multi-discipline
Date September
Distance 64km (40 miles)
Main obstacles Currents, technical
Website www.otillo.se
They call it Ö till Ö is a unique race in a unique environment.

Competitors say
❝Completely unique and a true journey from start to finish.❞

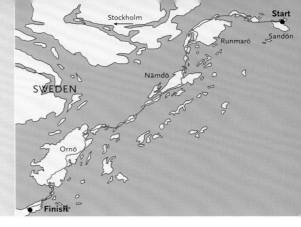

Ö till Ö

Traversing the length of a Swedish archipelago, competitors in the Ö till Ö must swim and run the 64km (40 miles) against a strict time limit, in a true test of endurance and versatility.

below Swimming ability is one of the keys to success in the Ö till Ö

Like all of the best things in life, the Ö till Ö (which literally translates as 'Island to Island') started life as a drunken bet. The goal was to see whether it was possible to get from Sandhamm (east of Stockholm) to Utö via some 18 islands surrounded by the Baltic Sea. This was to be completed by human power alone (i.e. by swimming and running), carrying all the gear and equipment needed to complete the challenge along the way. It took the first competitors two days to finish the course, and in the few years that

followed only a handful of teams managed to finish the race in its entirety.

Everything about the Ö till Ö is set up to challenge the athletes who take it on. Competitors in teams of two have just 14 hours to make the journey from north to south, swimming in total 10km (6 miles) and running 54km (34 miles). Along the way they can expect to enter and exit the water up to 38 times. And because the race takes place in September the water temperature can be variable, ranging from 10°C to 16°C (50–61°F). What's more – and one of the key challenges in the event – is that whatever an athlete starts the race with, they have to finish with.

Despite the multiple entry and exit points between the islands of the archipelago, there is no transition area with volunteers ready to collect and manage athletes' equipment. As such, athletes run and swim with everything they need. The most popular strategy in this respect is for athletes to swim in the running shoes that they start the race in and run in wetsuits. Wetsuits are mandatory items for all athletes to wear in the water (due to the water temperature), and the time taken to change in and out of them is prohibitive. Because of this, most teams opt to use a 'shortie' triathlon

wetsuit, warm enough to protect them against the cold,
flexible enough to allow them to run across an island.

To help them on their way, competitors also have the
option of using hand paddles and fins. The hand paddles are,
in part, there to protect the athletes climbing over the rocks
on their exit from the water, and many competitors choose to
wear them for the duration of the race. The fins, meanwhile,
offer obvious benefits in the water (particularly over shoes).
However, any time savings on the swim from the use of fins
is most likely to be offset by the time it takes to put them
on and take them off at every entry and exit point.

While the carrying and use of hand paddles and fins is
optional, certain things are compulsory. Every team must
carry a first-aid kit, compass, whistles and wetsuits. While
there are feed stations along the route, many will also carry
nutrition and hydration. All of this has to fit into a rucksack
that is waterproof but also appropriate for swimming.

And that is another of the unique challenges of the race.
Athletes must get used to swimming wearing not only a
pair of shoes but also a rucksack on their backs. This is all

the more important when you consider the swim conditions
along the race route. Swim sections in the race vary from
100m to 1600m (328–5250 feet). Because the water is
moving through channels between islands, the currents can
be strong and the waves not only irregular but occasionally
large. As such, and regardless of how strong a swimmer the
competitor is, there are certain island crossings on the route
that can present huge challenges.

These challenges are made all the more extreme because
of the team element involved in the race. At no point can a
team (of two) be more than 10m (33 feet) apart in the water.
On land, the distance between teammates can never be
more than 100m (328 feet). This can lead to situations where
team members attach themselves to one another, with the
stronger swimmer or runner literally dragging the weaker
athlete along.

Needless to say, to traverse the islands the athletes have
to be able to run. The fragmented nature of the run sections,
54km (34 miles) across trails and gravel paths, makes it all
the more difficult to settle into a rhythm, let alone allow the

body to adapt fully to one discipline or another. This could explain the relatively high dropout rate along the course. In 2011, only 59 of the 96 teams finished the race.

But that is the challenge of the Ö till Ö. A unique event, it challenges competitors like no other race and pits them against some of the most spectacular nature in Scandinavia. To complete the race, those who enter must not only master their environment but also adapt to the challenges and conditions that confront them. As such, it is racing in its most exhilirating and potentially rewarding form.

Antti Antonov

We (my team mate Bjorn Englund and I) won the race in 2011, breaking the course record in the process. My background is in triathlons, having qualified for Hawaii twice, with a best Ironman time of 8 hours, 48 minutes.

In preparation for the Ö till Ö we focused on some key areas, one of the most important of which was to practise entering and exiting the water. With 38 transitions in the race – out of the sea, over the rocks, onto the islands and back in again – a half minute lost at each point can add up to a significant time loss during the day. The other area we focused on was practising swimming in shoes, as you don't get as much propulsion with them on. I also swam with paddles a lot, as we would use these in the race and it can strain the shoulders. Even now, two months after the event, my shoulder still aches from using them for 11km (7 miles) of the race!

The one other area to improve was our trail-running ability and running on rough terrain similar to the islands. This event would best suit an ex-swimmer turned orienteer! As I live in Stockholm, there is plenty of opportunity to train on the archipelago and in lakes around the area.

One of the biggest challenges can be the water temperature, which a couple of years ago turned from 18°C (64°F) at the beginning of the week to 11°C (52°F) after a storm just before race day. This is compounded by the fact that most competitors use shortie wetsuits to make the running easier.

The biggest competition in 2011 was against Jonas Colting and Bjorn Andersson, who are two world-class long-distance triathletes and were favourites for the race. We figured they would be a lot quicker than us at swimming but slower on the trail running and this is how the race turned out, as we aimed to maintain contact through the early stages. Then Jonas and Bjorn dropped out due to sickness and so we continued to build a comfortable lead on the rest of the field.

It was still a tough race, though, as we began to get very tired and feel sick from the seawater, but we wanted to prove that we were still worthy winners even though the favourites had dropped out, so we pushed on for the course record.

Our next challenge is to improve this record; we believe we can go 15–20 minutes faster as we learn more about the event. One of our keys to success is to have fun in our team as we are racing, and we have a great partnership. The Ö till Ö is a 'gentleman's race' – very competitive, but with good-natured rivalry between teams. We have our plan of how to go quicker, but I'm not going to share that here!

Antti Antonov was one half of the team that won the Ö till Ö in 2011.

Type Bike
Date August
Distance 736km (453 miles)
Main obstacles Elevation change
Website www.hauteroute.org
They call it The world's toughest cycle sportive

Competitors say
The race requires a strong mental approach, to keep grinding up the cols every day when you're feeling exhausted.

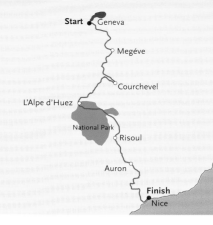

Start Geneva
Megéve
Courchevel
L'Alpe d'Huez
National Park Risoul
Auron
Finish Nice

La Haute Route

Seven days, 730km (454 miles) of cycling, and some of the toughest mountains the Alps have to offer – La Haute Route lays claim to being the world's toughest cycle sportive, and for very good reason.

below The competition is both brutal and unforgiving

In the mid-nineteenth century, a team of British Alpine experts pioneered a route from Chamonix to Zermatt. Crossing some of the toughest, most challenging peaks the Alps have to offer, 'The High Level Route' was a feat mastered on foot first, and then on skis, in 1911, when the name was changed to the French: 'Haute Route'. Nowadays, Haute Route has become a more generic term referring to any multi-day, high Alpine trek. But in the world of cycling, La Haute Route means just one thing: seven testing days in the Alps.

Always starting in Geneva and finishing in Nice, the course changes from year to year, but the length and difficulty remain the same. Cyclists can expect a race of up to 730km (453 miles), which boasts anything up to 17,000m (55,774 feet) of climbing. Along the way, competitors tackle classic routes ridden by legends of the Tour de France, and traverse cols that push the best riders in the world to the very limits of their endurance.

The names – and challenges – of these cols are legendary. At nearly 2000m (6561 feet), the Col de Madeleine boasts a 19km (12-mile) road to the summit, with an average gradient of eight per cent. Similarly, the Col du Telegraphe is a climb 12km (7 miles) long with an average gradient of 7.3 per cent; and the Galibier – with a height of 2645m (8678 feet) – boasts an 18km (11-mile) road with an average gradient of 6.9 per cent. As if that isn't enough, these cols can constitute just one day – and stage – of riding on the seven-day course.

Admittedly, at 160km (99 miles) that stage is by far the longest – and

arguably the hardest – of the race. For the most part, the race stages vary between 80 and 120km (50–75 miles). But that doesn't mean that the other stages are 'easy'. Far from it. Every stage of La Haute Route boasts at least two sizable climbs, and as the days and miles pass in the saddle the difficulty of each climb increases.

The sheer volume of climbing plays a key role in determining the challenges faced by competitors in La Haute Route. Covering that many vertical miles, as well as dealing with the physiological affect of riding at altitude, places a significant strain on the body. And it is coping with that strain over a number of days that becomes the most challenging factor in completing the race.

For, apart from the climbing and the altitude, it is the number of stages that make the race a real challenge. Just like the pros in le Tour de France, riders must complete a

above Good descending technique is important to a successful race

right A spectacle not a million miles away from the Tour de France

stage, recover and then do the same distance – or further – the next day (and the next) for seven consecutive days. As such, every rider has to be able to recover effectively so that they are physically and mentally capable of completing the next stage – and the race. As the days wear on, so the challenge to master their effective recovery increases. Failure to do so can lead a rider to 'crack' on one of the major climbs, or simply 'bonk' in the latter miles of a stage, and so lose a significant amount of time – and even jeopardise the chances of finishing. As such, athletes in the race have to master both their racing and their recovery fuelling and hydration.

What's more, for cyclists who have never ridden in the Alps, the technical aspects of mountain riding must be mastered quickly. Because, while the stated challenge of the race is the ability to conquer some commanding cols, the simple fact is that what goes up must come down, and descending some of these cols is as treacherous as the climbing is taxing. Not only are the descents long, steep and technically challenging, but having a 'peloton' of riders in close proximity means that every participant in the race must maintain control of both their speed and their line at all times. For anyone who has seen the crashes on the descents of the Tour de France, no explanation is necessary as to why crashing at speed on these roads is not a good idea.

But those tackling La Haute Route tend to be seasoned riders. With a field that attracts amateurs and semi-pros alike, and riders between the ages of 20 and 70, there is a huge variance in the speed of the field. To mitigate the risks associated with that, riders have a cut-off for each stage, calculated on an average peloton speed of 15km/h (9mph). Anyone falling outside that cut-off is declassified from the stage, but can continue in the race under their own steam. Needless to say, not everyone completes the race, and on average 10 per cent of the field fail to make it to the finish line in Nice.

But amid the pain and the fatigue, there is the spectacle. La Haute Route is not only one of the toughest cycle sportives on the planet but also one of the most picturesque. Those who compete in the race are rewarded with stunning mountain views at the top of some of cycling's most iconic climbs. It is as close as many mere mortals will get to the speed and exhilaration of the Tour de France, and the dull ache in the legs is carried away by an experience riders will never forget.

Mark Turner

I'm fairly new to cycling, having only really started road biking in 2006. Saying that, I have a background in endurance sports, including completing the Race to the South Pole. Since 2006, I'd done L'Etape du Tour several times but never a stage race.

In preparation for La Haute Route I was fairly time-limited, so focused on the quality of training over quantity, which was helped by living in Chamonix and having access to loads of great mountain climbs. I also rode on my own a lot, instead of getting any drafting benefit, which also added to the quality.

When it came to the race, I found the hardest part was the physical and mental wear and tear over the course of the week. The body got gradually sorer and particularly the first climb of every day was a struggle to get back into a rhythm. Day Three is the monster stage, which daunted everyone – even the top guys – especially with two stages prior to that. Some people got stronger as the week went on and some got weaker if they went too hard or didn't fuel or recover sufficiently. The other challenge was keeping all my gear organised as we moved between stages.

One of the biggest factors in the race was having the pressure of riding to a time limit every day. It was always at the back of your mind and makes a huge difference to how you feel, and forces you to push every day and keep an eye on the time. Maintaining a consistent pace and managing your body over the race is important; it is easy to push hard one day when you're feeling good or someone makes a break, but consistent pacing is important.

As is keeping fuelled correctly, understanding what the body needs and what it can process as the week develops. What you start off eating might change towards the end of the week as the body tires of energy gels.

We were lucky, as throughout the race it was beautiful sunny weather. Being in the Alps, though, this could easily have changed for the worse and made the week even tougher. Riding at altitude was an issue for some, although my base in Chamonix really helped for this.

The race requires a strong mental approach, to keep grinding up the cols every day when you're feeling exhausted. This shared effort, though, creates some strong unspoken bonds, and there was a great feeling at the finish, with a lot of emotion and relief. It was an amazing achievement to complete such a stunning week.

Mark Turner is Executive Chairman of the organisers of La Haute Route and has previously completed the inaugural race and the Race to the South Pole.

Type Multi-discipline
Date Throughout year
Distance 467km (290 miles)
Main obstacles Cold, mental, distance
Website www.enduroman.com
They call it The most gruelling and the most challenging endurance event known to man.

Competitors say
If you were to choose to run to Dover, swim the English Channel or cycle to Paris, most people would question your sanity. However, an elite group of endurance athletes have chosen to do all three in what must be the world's toughest triathlon.

Enduroman Arch to Arc

They are two iconic monuments that capture moments in the rich history of Europe: London's Marble Arch and the Arc de Triomphe in Paris attract tourists (and traffic) from miles around. But these days, these historic monuments are more than simply giant photo opportunities surrounded by passing motorists; they mark the start and end point of one of Europe's – and the world's – toughest endurance events. An event so challenging that only nine people in the history of the race have completed it, and until 2011 no woman had ever mastered the course.

And what a course. As soon as the hand of the athlete leaves Marble Arch, the clock begins. What follows is an immense feat of human endurance. It begins with a 140km (87-mile) run from the centre of London to the shores of Dover. Next, the athlete takes to the water and swims ~35km (~22 miles) across the English Channel. Finally, having reached the shores of Calais they mount their bike and cycle 291km (181 miles) to Paris. Physically challenging, mentally exhausting and psychologically taxing, the Arch to Arc forces even the toughest athletes to search their souls and pool their resources if they are to stand a chance of completing this legendary challenge.

What makes it so tough? Where do we start? Probably at the beginning, because training for this sort of event is difficult. To master one ultra-distance discipline is hard enough, but to master three is nigh-on impossible. In doing this, athletes have to manage not only the physical but also the mental aspect of their preparation, making sure that they do not burn out in the months and weeks leading up to the event.

The logistics around the event are far from simple as well. The timing and dates of the challenge are largely determined by the tides within the English Channel. These tides have a significant impact on anyone attempting to cross the Straits of Dover, so every effort must be made to ensure that the runner arrives in Dover with enough time to rest and recuperate before setting off on the swim. As such,

right Crossing the Channel is undoubtedly the most daunting leg

left Unlike many races, athletes take the roads as they come: busy!

the athlete must start the run from London to Dover within 48 hours of the pre-determined swim time.

And this run is no mean feat. At 140km (87 miles), it is further than the average ultra-marathon, and large sections of it take place overnight. The run is completed under the pressure of knowing what comes next: the need to conserve energy and with the goal of reaching Dover with plenty of time prior to the start of the swim.

Swimming the English Channel is, in itself, a challenge worthy of the pages of this book. To do it as the middle leg of an already tough triathlon verges on madness. Unlike the standalone swim, competitors are allowed to swim in a wetsuit, giving advantages of buoyancy and some warmth. But wetsuits offer no protection against the tides that surge through the English Channel. These tides play a huge role in determining the speed at which the crossing can take place – and, of course, the resultant energy expenditure. The organisers of the event charter a piloted boat, which will not

only facilitate the optimum route dependent on the tides but also help swimmers steer clear of ferries, yachts and commercial cargo ships in one of the busiest shipping lanes in the world. What's more, to ensure a successful crossing the swimmer must maintain a good speed. Failure to do so means that they will invariably get caught up in a turning tide, which will exponentially increase the time it takes to complete the swim.

Swimmers must keep moving, not only to fight off the cold but also to ensure they are in a position to attempt the final leg: the cycle into Paris. While 291km (181 miles) is within the capabilities of most strong cyclists, doing this off the back of an ultra-distance marathon and one of the world's toughest swims ensures that it is far from easy. Psychologically the two hardest parts of the race are over. But keeping the legs ticking over can be draining, and when mental and physical fatigue combine in a race like this, it is easy for competitors to be beaten by their own heads.

Not to mention the time limit. The cut-off for the race is 168 hours (seven days), but this can be extended if weather and tidal conditions in the English Channel necessitate it. Within those seven days, athletes have to include time for rest (most will sleep between the three disciplines) and need to deal with the cumulative build-up of fatigue. Needless to say, the speed at which the course has been completed is frighteningly fast. The current record is held by Eddie Ette at an incredible 81 hours, 5 minutes. In 2011, Rachael Cadman became the first female athlete to complete the race, finishing in 97 hours, 37 minutes.

The combination of three tests of ultra-endurance makes this a brutal examination of some of the strongest athletes in the world. In so doing it quite justifiably earns the distinction of being the toughest triathlon out there.

Rachael Cadman

The hardest thing about the Arch to Arc is trying to motivate yourself for the 18 months you have to train prior to race. During the race itself, it isn't hard to motivate yourself – this is what you've been building for and you just get on with it. But the training is hard. I was doing all of my own training plans, and when you do that there is always the concern that you are doing it totally wrong. That's where the intermediary races really helped because you realise that you did it and that you are on track. Doing this was a real learning experience – it became my own little psychology and physiology study all about me.

Although there were high and low points, during the race it wasn't difficult to find motivation somewhere.

I started the run on a Friday afternoon and it was really hot. I'm always pretty grumpy for about the first 32km (20 miles) of a run, but I was distracted running through London, which was good. I've found that I perform much better at night, and from 32 to 64 km (20–40 miles) I felt great. Obviously, I started to deteriorate a little bit, but it wasn't until 97km (60 miles) that I thought, 'This is really tough now.' I wasn't built to run 140km (87 miles) – I have a swimmer's build – so I struggled a bit.

If I'm honest, the best bit of the whole four days was finishing the run, getting into an ice bath, then getting into bed and eating a Subway!

The first six hours of the swim were difficult. The conditions were really poor and there were a number of times when the wind was blowing the boat too far away from me. Six hours in is when the night fell and I felt fine and the water got a lot calmer. Then, when the sun came up it looked like I was about 500m (1640 feet) from the shore. Two-and-a-half hours later (because of the current – the boat pilot thought it might take me six hours to fight through it), I was in Calais.

I really didn't want to start the bike because I was really tired, but once I set off I loved it! We had massive thunderstorms and I was drenched, but it was warm and I had a whale of a time.

Of course, the finish in Paris was amazing. I got told off because you're supposed to go underground to finish, but I didn't want to finish on an underpass so I cycled onto the roundabout, which is apparently a massive no-no. So at the end of the race everyone was yelling at me!

Rachael Cadman became the first woman to complete the Arch to Arc in 2011.

KEY FACTS

Type Canoe
Date April
Distance 201km (125 miles)
Main obstacles Currents, mental, technical
Website www.dwrace.org.uk
They call it The longest non-stop canoe race in the world.

Competitors say
'You know that every time you take a stroke it's one closer to Westminster; keep doing that and you'll get there eventually!!'

Devizes to Westminster International Canoe Race

A journey from the sleepy backwaters of England to the bustling metropolis that is London, the Devizes to Westminster Canoe race is a test of stamina and the ability to portage a canoe!

The longest non-stop race of its kind in the world, the Devizes to Westminster canoe race is quintessentially English. From its origins in a pub on the River Avon to the unique challenges faced by competitors in the race itself; from the sleepy towns and villages the river sidles through to its fast-flowing finish in the heart of one of the world's great cities, Devizes to London is not only a test of physical endurance but a fantastic journey through the heart of England.

The challenge of canoeing 201km (125 miles) non-stop is enough to test the mettle of even the most seasoned canoeists. But the race isn't as simple as paddling along a gently flowing river. The first 84km (52 miles) are on the Kennet & Avon Canal and the next 89km (55 miles) on the River Thames, which means competitors have to negotiate 77 portages (carrying the boat around a water obstacle) before the final section of the race. This final section is where they exit the non-tidal Thames and enter the 'real' river. Fierce tides, river traffic and plenty of flotsam and jetsam are waiting to greet the already weary competitors. Needless to say, not many people have the endurance and mental fitness to keep paddling through the night, stopping on a regular basis to carry their canoe around a lock (there are 35 locks within 32km/20 miles during one particularly arduous stretch), until finally finishing opposite the Houses of Parliament in Central London.

Although, for those who do, there is the knowledge that they have achieved something truly special.

left Competitors set off on a non-stop endurance challenge

below There aren't many more spectacular finish lines

As with all the best ideas, Roy Cooke dreamed up the concept of travelling from Devizes to Westminster in a pub on the Avon. Back in 1948, the canals on the route were largely derelict, but Cooke still attempted the journey. He didn't make it. However, hearing about his attempt at the trip a local group of Scouts thought that they would take on the challenge. And so, on the Easter weekend of 1948, this group set off, carrying all of their equipment in a bid to make it to London. The press attention around the expedition was unprecedented. Newspapers ran the story and the local cinemas interrupted performances to update people on their progress. Some 89 hours, 50 minutes after setting off, the Scouts pulled alongside the seat of the British government: the Houses of Parliament. The benchmark had been set.

In the years that followed, several crews attempted the route. The time set by the Scouts was repeatedly reduced until, in 1949, a crew representing Richmond Canoe Club completed the course in just over 49 hours. With the continuing interest shown by racers, one of the competitors from the club decided to organise the event as an annual

above River traffic presents yet another obstacle

contest. In Easter 1950, 17 boats took part in the first official race, with Richmond Canoe Club winning again in just under 35 hours. The British armed forces viewed the race as an opportunity for training and won the race from 1951 to 1970 (apart from the year 1952) with teams from the Parachute Regiment, Royal Marines, SAS and Special Forces.

The rules were changed in 1971, so that canoes did not have to carry food and camping kit and the use of support teams to supply food and drink was allowed. The current course record under these new rules was set in 1979 at an impressive 15 hours, 34 minutes.

To achieve that sort of time, competitors have to paddle constantly through the night. And that is one of the greatest challenges of the race. Some 90 per cent of retirements from the race happen between Henley and Windsor, around 96km (60 miles) in, as darkness starts to fall and the river winds its dark way through the countryside. And it gets cold. The average temperature in England at that time of year ranges from 6 to 13°C (42–55°F). To maintain forward momentum through a cold (and usually wet) night is exhausting both physically and mentally.

What's more, that momentum is repeatedly interrupted because of the need to portage the 77 locks that stand between Devizes and Teddington (the gateway to the final tidal section of the race). At every one of these locks, competitors have to lift both themselves and their canoe out of the water, carry it to the next launch point and start again. This would be entirely bearable if it were to happen just once or twice, but over the course of the race, competitors lift and launch their boat up to 154 times. Every effort disrupts momentum, interrupts concentration, and places additional levels of fatigue on already weary limbs.

Needless to say, when competitors do eventually pass through the locks, the challenges do not end, they merely change. One of the fastest-flowing tidal rivers through a capital city, the 29km (18-mile) stretch from Teddington to the Houses of Parliament will see competitors fighting a bitter battle against a strong tide and choppy water.

Of course, if the tide is in their favour it is relatively plain sailing. But reach Teddington at an unfavourable turning point, and the energy required to maintain forward momentum increases exponentially.

For those who conquer these peculiarly English obstacles, the reward is a berth aside one of the greatest buildings in the world. And once the muscles have recovered and the fatigue subsided, there is the knowledge of having conquered one of the toughest canoe races the world has to offer.

Chris Wingham

I did the race in 2007 with a fellow Army Officer, Phil Hobbs. We finished the race in 28 hours, 1 minute and I was absolutely thrilled to successfully complete it. Not because of our time but because I never expected to complete it. The reason for that was our poor level of preparation, mainly as a result of a last-minute decision to enter the race and with absolutely no paddling experience between us. People who had done the race before, told us that we were idiots for attempting it and that we'd never finish.

I guess that actually made us more determined to get through it, and by race day I think we would have swum the 200km (125 miles) towing our boat behind us if it came to it!

We knew it would be tough, but as we were both serving in the Army we were used to being on arduous physical exercises for long periods of time where we were cold, wet and tired. Perfect preparation! Physically we were both training every day in the gym (mainly cardiovascular and upper-body work) and paddling as much as we could (I'd say probably four times a week on average – which, as I've said, was woefully inadequate!).

For us, the biggest obstacle was learning to paddle. The boats that you race in are not your usual, nice, stable kayaks! They are specifically designed for racing and are therefore very thin, streamlined and inherently unstable. We spent at least two months in January and February capsizing, and really suffering from the cold. This had a massive effect on the time that we could spend training, as after an hour we were just too cold to continue.

Other big obstacles that you need to overcome are paddling in the dark (as you paddle all night) and in choppy waters (once you get to Teddington, you start to travel along the Thames, which is not a nice, flat water surface). They just take practice, although little things like sticking reflective strips on the back of the front man's paddles help to keep your paddling rhythm.

The biggest problem we had was actually half a mile (800m) from the finish line when we capsized in the Thames. As I've said before, the water gets very choppy, especially with other big boats using the river, but you want to utilise the current to best effect – i.e. in the middle of the river. The problem here is that if you do capsize you have a long swim to get to the shore and drain your boat before getting in again. Probably not a problem for competent crews, but for novices it's definitely worth considering the line that you take down the river Thames.

To complete it was amazing, as we never expected to finish. It also felt great to tell people who had said we were nuts for trying with such little experience. So, on reflection I'm really proud to have done it despite the unimpressive time.

Chris Wingham is an ultra-endurance athlete, and completed Devizes to Westminster in 2007.

Type Swim
Date Year-round
Distance 32 km (21 miles) – although variable
Main obstacles Distance, currents, cold, mental
Website www.channelswimmingassociation.com
They call it The Everest of open-water swimming.

Competitors say

❝ I used to treat the Channel swims as a day's work. I'd tell the boss the day before I wouldn't be in the next day, and then would return to work the following day after the swim.❞

UNITED KINGDOM

Dover

Folkestone

Start

ENGLISH CHANNEL

Finish

Wissant

FRANCE

English Channel Swim

The English Channel is one of the busiest shipping straits in the world, and its fierce tides and relentless cold make a swim crossing one of the iconic ultra-endurance events.

below No wetsuits allowed!

In 1875, Captain Matthew Webb took to the waters of the Straits of Dover in little more than a swimsuit, cap and pair of goggles. Some 21 hours and 45 minutes later, Webb was standing on the shores of Calais, having unwittingly laid the foundations for one of the world's iconic endurance challenges. During the course of his Channel swim, the strength of the tides forced Webb to breaststroke for five hours without making any progress and it is estimated that he actually swam some 64km (40 miles) in total to complete the crossing.

These days, most crossings are nearer the 32km (21-mile) mark. However, the challenges that face those who attempt to swim the Channel remain almost identical. It is not the distance that makes the challenge so tough (although that is without doubt an enormous factor). Rather, it is a combination of variables that are beyond the control of the swimmer.

The first of these is the cold. The waters of the English Channel typically range from 15 to 18°C (59–65°F) during the optimal months for the crossing (June to September). Under the Channel Swimming Association regulations, it is a non-wetsuit swim, meaning that for any crossing to be recognised a swimmer can use only a swimsuit, goggles, earplugs, two caps and some grease – for warmth. As such, it is imperative that anyone attempting the challenge has extensive experience of cold-water swimming to prepare their body for it.

While the weather in the Channel is difficult to predict, the tides are not. The Straits of Dover are susceptible to strong tidal flows, largely determined

opposite Beating the turning tide will improve the finishing time significantly

below Speed is largely determined by the skill of the navigator and strength of the tides

by the moon. With two favourable tidal movements per month, swimmers are able to pinpoint the optimum hour of the optimum day to begin the challenge. However, once under way they are in a race against time to cross the Channel before the tides turn again. This knowledge impacts every element of the swim, from the speed at which the challenge is tackled to the time taken on feed breaks. The impact of any miscalculation can be severe. Once the tides begin to turn, the strength of the water means that, like Webb, swimmers can expend a lot of energy battling simply maintaining their position in the water. Needless to say, the impact of the tide will be greater on slower swimmers, who are likely to end up swimming an 'S' or 'Z' shaped route between England and France. Any swimmer that can maintain a pace of 3km/h (1.8 mph) – including time taken for drink and nutrition – can expect 12–13 hours in the water.

The final, major variable that so often impacts a crossing is the presence of other vessels. The English Channel is one of the busiest shipping lanes in the world with over 600 commercial ship movements and 80–100 ferry crossings between Dover and Calais every day. These ships cannot alter course for a single swimmer, and so pilots and crew have to

help the athlete negotiate this 'highway' safely. With a skilled pilot, the risk may be somewhat mitigated. However, it is ever present, and the psychological effect of a ferry wash or cargo liner passing close by merely serves to add yet another strain on a taxing day.

That is why most of the individuals attempting to swim the Channel do so with the assistance of the Channel Swimming Association (CSA). The CSA have a list of endorsed pilots who help guide swimmers through the Channel, and can provide advice on times and dates to ensure the best chance of success. The CSA also provides advice on training and nutrition for the crossing, as well as keeping a historical database of all those who have completed the swim.

Despite the risks and challenges, the Channel Crossing is an increasingly popular benchmark in endurance sports. The most common – and shortest – route is the 31km (19-mile) 'hop' from Shakespeare Beach, Dover to Cap Gris Nez, the headland between Calais and Boulogne.

The fastest verified crossing of the channel was by the Bulgarian Petar Stoychev, who in 2007 crossed the stretch of water in 6 hours, 57 minutes, 50 seconds. On average most

swimmers take over 12 hours to complete the route, with the longest ever crossing just under 27 hours. British swimmer Alison Streeter holds the record for the most crossings: 43 trips across the channel, including seven in one year.

In terms of challenge, there aren't many greater than swimming the English Channel. The Everest of swimming is an apt name, and one that should inspire only the toughest and most dedicated of athletes. Completing the crossing places individuals in an elite club of supreme endurance athletes, a club that most people will never be able to join.

Michael Read

For my first swim across the Channel in 1969, I was really positive at the start as I had done a lot of preparation, including eight or nine double Windermeres, Loch Ness and Loch Lomond swims. My swimming background prior to this was also extensive (qualifying for the Olympic Games among many other swimming achievements). I strongly believed I could complete the Channel swim and everything went smoothly as planned.

In all my attempts, while there were jellyfish stings and seasickness, the biggest challenge I had was getting sponsorship to help pay for the attempt. I then had the pressure to keep the sponsors happy during the swim.

Initially I wasn't focused on getting the record for crossings. I was trying to do a double crossing, and after trying to achieve this I had completed a further five crossings. The closest I got to a double was just missing out in the last mile. I did a day's work, left at 7 p.m. to get to Dover, started swimming at 11 p.m. through the night and for just over 29 hours, before pulling out in the last mile, as I was exhausted and the tide was against me, so I wasn't making progress. I wish my crew had motivated me more instead of letting me get out, especially as I later learnt that the tide would have turned in three hours.

By now I had done six crossings, just short of the record, which was then improved further by an Australian swimmer. For the next few years, it was a game of cat and mouse as he would improve the record and I would keep up with him. He would fly over from Australia, swim the Channel perhaps three times and then go home

again. I would then match him – I once did three crossings in eight days – until he stopped coming over, and I took the record and started building a buffer.

I was always OK swimming in the cold. Once, during one of my slower crossings of just over 18 hours, the sea temperature was 12°C (55°F). This wasn't as bad as Loch Ness one year, where I swam for 14½ hours in 6°C (43°F). I became well acclimatised to colder temperatures by training in the 50m (160-foot) outdoor pool in Ipswich, and my mental strength kept me going in spite of the cold.

I've been lucky with injuries in my long career; I always competed very regularly and kept in good shape. I used to train 22 or 23 times a week when I was training for the Olympics; this was while still working full-time and having a family. I used to swim in the morning, at noon and in the evening. I've always coached myself, never having someone to bully me into training; I've always trained and swam just because I've wanted to.

I used to treat the Channel swims as a day's work. I'd tell the boss the day before I wouldn't be in the next day and then would return to work the following day after the swim. I still train five times a week, win medals in Masters competitions and do ultra-swims such as a recent 30km (19-mile) race.

I take a lot of pride in being a World Record Holder for number of crossings and being the current 'King of the Channel'.

Michael Read has swum the English Channel 33 times and is widely known as the 'King of the Channel'.

Type Bike
Date September
Distance 2173km (1350 miles)
Main obstacles Distance, mental
Website www.racearoundireland.com
They call it Europe's toughest cycling challenge

Competitors say
"A very serious undertaking, but with the right frame of mind is also still a fantastic adventure."

Race Around Ireland

A non-stop time trial around the circumference of the Emerald Isle, the Race Around Ireland lays claim to being one of the toughest cycling challenges in the world for very good reason.

right The stunning scenery is negotiated at high speed and under significant time pressure

One of the most picturesque countries in Europe, Ireland enjoys a reputation for not only its stunning scenery but the craic. And while the athletes in the Race Around Ireland will experience a limited amount of the latter, this brutal time trial exposes them to plenty of the former. Because at 2173km (1350 miles), the Race Around Ireland understandably lays claim to being one of the toughest cycling races in Europe.

Starting in Navan, County Meath, cyclists follow a predefined route through 19 time stations on their way to the finish line back in Navan. It is a complete circuit of both the Republic and Northern Ireland. Along the way competitors tackle 25 major climbs, can expect to sleep for as little as two hours per day and pass by numerous landmarks and legendary towns. What's more, those competing in the solo race have just 132 hours to complete the journey (there are also two-, four- and eight-man team options). There are strict time cut-offs along the route, and anyone failing to meet those cut-offs is eliminated from the race (unless a successful appeal is lodged with the race organisers).

And therein lies the inherent challenge of the race. Because to stand a fighting chance of completing the course cyclists – and their support teams – tackle the challenge knowing they can only afford a couple of hours of sleep per day. The stress that this places on the rider is immense, with sleep deprivation coupled with extreme physical exertion playing havoc with the mind. As such, it is up to the support crew to ensure that their rider not only maintains the pace required to reach the time stations, but has sufficient rest to be able to function while out on the road.

Because despite being a time trial no part of the course is closed to traffic. As a result, athletes have to negotiate towns and highways like any other cyclist. They also have to strictly adhere to the rules of the road. Failure to do so leads to penalties, and repeat offenders will ultimately be disqualified from the race.

The nature of the Race Around Ireland is very similar to the Race Across America. Every cyclist has to be aided by at least one support car (solo riders are recommended to take two). This support team plays a hugely important part in the race. First and foremost they are the navigators for the cyclists. While many of the roads around Ireland are well

right Climbing has its benefits!

signposted, the race takes in a number of smaller towns and villages where signs can be few and far between (or simply non-existent). As such, most teams will have a dedicated navigator to ensure the cyclist does not add any additional miles to their already arduous journey. This team is also responsible for managing the nutrition and hydration of the athlete, as well as overseeing their rest. Indeed, because of the strain that the race places on the teams, race organisers check both the athletes and the teams for signs of fatigue at various stages. At any point during the race an organiser can force a team to take a four-hour break if they are deemed too tired.

But of course the fatigue of the team is nothing compared to that of the athlete. The physical challenge of time-trialling this kind of distance goes without saying. What's more, many cyclists will train their bodies in the weeks and days leading up to the event to achieve sufficient levels of deep sleep in a short period of time. But while cyclists can prepare for the physicality of the event, there are some factors they cannot control.

The September weather in Ireland is changeable to say the least. Temperatures can vary from 4–15°C (40–60°F) and conditions out on the road can be tempestuous. Rain is almost guaranteed on the course, and at times vicious head and side winds blow hard enough to make keeping the bike on the road a challenge. This becomes a significant factor when competing on a time trial bike, because a TT-rig with a disc wheel on a windy road is hard to manage. And that's before spending three, four or five days in the saddle.

Like so many of the challenges in this book, the Race Around Ireland attracts some truly elite athletes who lay down some impressive times. In 2009 only four people completed the race, Joe Barr winning in 108 hours 12 minutes. Bernd Paul led home the six finishers in 2010 in 113 hours 12 minutes, and Valerio Zamboni was the first of just two finishers in 2011 in 131 hours and 36 minutes. It's difficult to compare the times like for like as elements of the course change from year to year, but these are cyclists with strong pedigrees and those are solid times.

The Race Around Ireland challenges the strongest cyclists mentally and physically. To complete it a competitor must conquer a lack of sleep as well as sustain a strong pace on the bike for mile after mile, hour after hour and day after day. To do so is a true challenge and places those cyclists in an elite group of athletes.

Valerio Zamboni

ATHLETE PERSPECTIVE

A race like the Race Around Ireland requires some prior body and psychological preparation. Training your body is the easiest part of the job. I usually do intervals for three days a week of no more than three hours each, and long climbs during the weekend of around five-hours. For this race I just had to switch one day of the weekend to short and very steep climbs. Of course, I was already training with long rides (10 to 12 hours) every two or three weeks and other ultra-long races have been done during the season.

The toughest part is on the mental level: you have to have a lot of self-confidence and come to the race very well motivated with a primary goal in mind. If your main objective is to finish the race or even win the race, you have to adapt your pace accordingly to what you have decided beforehand.

Fighting for the victory means pushing your resources to their limits. If you cannot do it you have to consider a DNF. During the race you spend dozens of hours purely thinking about your strategy and how to keep your pace up and thinking about different subjects sometimes helps you to keep going. In my case, I tend to slightly slow my speed down and try to focus exclusively on the race.

During the first 24–30 hours the weather was so bad that my 'surviving mode' was activated, and I was not really aiming for a place in the ranking. During the second day the weather gave us a moment of peace from time to time, and a lot of riders decided to take a short break. This was a crucial moment where I had to decide whether I wanted try to win the race or just finish it.

After discussions with my trainer, I chose to keep going in order to save a sleep cycle in comparison to the other riders. From that point on the only thing I had to do was to understand my immediate follower's sleeping pattern and stay on the bike a few more hours after he stopped to rest. After four days I exactly matched my sleeping pattern with my closest participant's. By doing so, I ended up finishing the race eight hours before the guy who took second.

Of course, when you race like this some strange things can happen, including hallucinations. Over the first three days I only slept for a total of 186-minutes and sleep deprivation started to take over my mind. I went through a terrible night with hallucinations for hours. Yellow flowers start to morph into the form of gnomes, who came from the edge of the road to its middle in order to attack me: I knew perfectly well that it was not true, but the feeling was not pleasant at all!

Valerio Zamboni won the 2011 Race Around Ireland.

Type Bike
Date February
Distance 600km (373 miles)
Main obstacles Terrain, weather, technical
Website www.ironbike.it
They call it The Legend – the world's hardest
mountain bike race

Competitors say
*'It's steeper, longer, more technical
than anything I've done before.'*

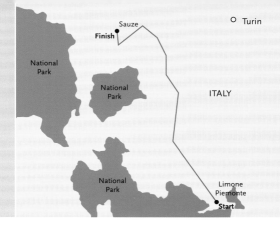

Iron Bike

Some 600km (373 miles) long and boasting 27,000m (88,580 feet) of climbing, the Iron Bike challenges
even the hardiest mountain bike experts on a gruelling trek into the heart of the Italian Alps.

The wind whips against your face. You're tired. You've spent the last five days tackling one of the fiercest races on the planet. In the process you've climbed more than twice the height of Mount Everest and become the master of your own mental and physical fatigue. As you cycle up and up into the clouds, up and up towards yet another towering summit, the temperature plummets. You stretch your fingers, trying desperately to get the blood flowing because you know you're going to need them. Soon. At the top of

this summit is a hair-raising descent into the valley below. And, at its most dangerous point, that descent is down a very long, very steep staircase.

That is the occasionally nonsensical reality of the Iron Bike, a journey through the heart of the Italian Alps. It is raw, it is tough and, at times, it is dangerous. And that is why it attracts some of the best mountain bikers in the world. Because it is a true test of physical, mental and technical prowess. And it is relentless.

below The views
are nothing short
of breathtaking

Taking place over eight stages and involving more than 27,000m (88,580 feet) of vertical climbing, competitors in the Iron Bike are forced to tackle everything that the Alps can throw at them. And there are no easy stages. From the outset, competitors are pushed to the limits, climbing 3500m (11,500 feet) over 100km (62 miles) of variable – and often technically challenging – terrain. In the days that follow, the riders will routinely bag 4000m (13,000 feet) of climbing per day. The climbs are difficult – the 2000m (6500 feet) ascent to the summit of Mount Chaberton (3131m/10,200 feet) is a particular highlight – and the terrain and conditions vary dramatically. All of this makes preparing for – and competing in – the Iron Bike so tough. The race boasts back-to-back stages of a distance and physicality that is almost impossible to replicate.

Unlike road biking, mountain biking is as much about technical skill as it is about physical prowess. And with every ascent – however tough these may be – there is a descent on the other side. Of course, some of these descents are fun, easy and a pleasure to ride. But some are incredibly technical, requiring mental forethought and excellent bike handling skills simply to stay on two wheels. And those are the ones that are rideable. One infamous descent (open only if conditions allow) involves tackling a precarious mountainside staircase. Needless to say, riding is optional. However, even walking this staircase presents unique challenges, as riders not only have to carry their bike but must do so in mountain-bike shoes, which are far from optimised for stair-walking.

Of course, that is before the weather is taken into account. As with any mountain race, the weather in the Italian Alps can deteriorate rapidly. As such, riders must be prepared to tackle any weather, and also be technically proficient at handling their bikes in changeable conditions. And as any seasoned rider will attest, entering a greasy rock garden en route to the valley that lies beyond the summit of a 3000m (9800 feet) mountain with aching, battered and bruised joints can be tough – on both the human and the bike. The sheer technicality of the terrain also presents riders with mechanical issues. As such, every competitor needs to ensure that they start the race with the right kit, knowledge of bike mechanics and – for some – a support person to keep their bike in shape.

Needless to say, the Iron Bike is set up to challenge the faculties on every level. But it is also designed to give riders the opportunity to experience terrain and conditions that they would rarely otherwise see. Whether that be epic vistas over the Alps, or the thrill of tackling the 2.5km (1.5-mile) mine shaft on the race route, the experience is unique.

Of course, at the end of each stage there is a certain amount of rest and relaxation afforded to the riders. But athletes do not expect five-star accomodation, nor do they receive it. Like the course itself, the home comforts are good, but basic. All of these factors could explain why so few competitors actually complete the race. Of the 140 who set out in 2011, less than 50 crossed the finishing line. In comparison to many races in this book, that is a high drop-out rate.

Beautifully challenging on numerous levels, the Iron Bike is a true test for even the strongest riders in the world. Not only pushing them physically, it also demands mental and technical prowess that most people would be simply incapable of achieving. And it does it in an environment that is as stunning as it is harsh.

Matt Page

To be honest, going into Iron Bike I didn't know how to prepare for the race because I didn't know what to expect. With hindsight, I would prepare by just going out for long days in the saddle, trying to get as much technical riding as possible and a bit of carrying your bike, as there's quite a bit of 'hike-a-bike'.

It was a lot harder than I thought it would be, though. I was expecting it to be hard, as I had heard a lot of things about it – people were saying that it is the hardest race in the world. But it was the first stage race I'd entered, so I wasn't sure how I was going to be day to day or how I was going to be during the race.

Day-to-day recovery was definitely the hardest part. Each day was absolutely solid, and harder than anything I've ever done before. So to do seven days back-to-back was really tough. The first few days when I woke up and thought about what I had to do, and that I still had another five or six days left, I was wondering if I could get through it. That was the hardest bit.

During the race, the climbs just seemed never-ending. You'd go over one climb and then drop down and then you'd go over another and another and another. You didn't really get time to think about anything because you constantly had the next climb on your mind. One day, for example, if I was going to explain it to someone who knows the UK, it started off with a 1000m (3280 feet) ascent, which was equivalent to a cross-country race up and down Snowdon. But then you still had another 70km (44 miles) with 3000–4000m (9840–13,120 feet) of climbing to do after that. The figures that you're talking about just don't add up in terms of UK riding – you just can't do enough climbing in this country. It's steeper, longer, more technical – just bigger and harder than anything I've done before.

The atmosphere in the race is competitive, but it's friendly as well. You're all in the same boat and it isn't easy for anyone – even the people winning are pushing themselves to the limit. So there's a big mutual respect between everyone who finishes it. And everyone is there to finish: even the leaders are there to finish the race before they even think about winning it. The guy who was leading dropped out on the penultimate day, which just goes to show that nobody has an easy ride, and if you're not feeling 100 per cent there's no point in carrying on. It's just too hard and there is no easy day.

Matt Page finished fifth at the 2011 Iron Bike – his first race on the course. Matt has won numerous national and international mountain bike races. For more on Matt visit: blog.wiggle.com/author/mattpage/.

ATHLETE PERSPECTIVE

Type Foot | **Date** August
Distance 80km (50 miles)
Main obstacles Elevation change, altitude
Website www.themountainman.ch
They call it A brutal and beautiful 80km (50 miles) race
with 5000m (16,400 feet) of literally breathtaking
climbs in the heart of Switzerland.

Competitors say
❝It was hot, long and steep!❞

SWITZERLAND

Pilatus · Finish
Sarnen
Engleberg
Start

The Mountainman

Snow-capped peaks, rolling fields and turquoise blue lakes provide a welcome distraction for competitors in one of Europe's toughest trail races.

below Stunning, if not slightly perilous

The landscape of the Swiss Alps attracts visitors from all over the world. Some come to meander through the fields, others to scale the peaks that tower up from the lush valley floors. And for one very special weekend each year, a select few come to tackle one of the toughest ultra-marathon trail races in Europe.

Taking place every August, the Mountainman ultra-distance race pits athletes against 80km (50 miles) of tough trail running. During the course of the event, athletes can expect to climb more than 5000 vertical metres (16,400 feet), and descend nearly 4700m (15,400 feet). At its peak, the course hits 2323m (7621 feet), with athletes never dropping

below 968m (3175 feet). In addition to the physical strain of tackling long, hard ascents and descents, athletes are forced to deal with the affects of altitude – a potentially dangerous variable to factor into the race.

Starting at Trubsee in the shadow of Mount Titlis, the course immediately climbs to the highest point on the route, the 2323m (7621-foot) Jochpass. From there, the climbing and descending remains relatively constant (and always above 2000m/6500 feet) until the competitors drop to the lowest point of the course, the Bruningpass. One long ascent follows the descent into the Bruningpass, and after summiting the Schonbuel, athletes face a stretch of course

that sits comfortably above the 1500m (4920-foot) mark. One last little peak follows before the final climb up to Pilatus Kulm, the finishing point. Along the way, competitors are treated to some of the picture-perfect sights of the Swiss Alps, including deep blue mountain lakes, towering rock faces, and some spectacular views of the mountains.

Not that they have time to appreciate them, because competitors must meet the strict cut-off times. Athletes have eight-and-a-half hours to reach the lowest point

left The support
the athletes receive
at the finish makes
it all worth it.

opposite The
mountains provide an
incredible backdrop

on the course at the Bruningpass, just beyond the 30km (18-mile) mark. They then have another four hours to nail the next 30km (18 miles) and reach Langis, and a further two to reach Lutoldsmatt, the basepoint of the final climb to Pilatus Kulm. For non-elite runners, there's a good chance that night will have fallen by this point, and the final run up to the summit of Pilatus Kulm will be played out in the dark. Those near the back of the field have just 16 hours, 30 minutes to reach the finish line. Anyone who fails to make these cut-off times is allowed to continue, but not as part of the race. These time scales are indicative of the challenges facing competitors in the Mountainman.

The race is, for the most part, run above 1500m (5000 feet). While not physically that high, the effect of prolonged periods of severe exertion on the body at this kind of altitude can be severe. Headaches, light-headedness, dizziness or drowsiness are not uncommon among those not used to exercising at altitude. And the demands of the race are severe. The sheer volume of ascending and descending causes massive strain, not only on the legs but on the heart and the lungs as well. As such, to complete the race, athletes must be able to manage not only their physical but also their mental strength.

Add into the mix the changeable nature of weather conditions in the Alps, and you begin to see why the Mountainman has such an exhaustive list of recommended equipment and contingency plans should things go wrong. All athletes have to carry a basic first-aid kit, clothes and equipment should the weather turn in the mountains, and a mobile phone to be able to call in emergencies. In the event of emergencies, there are regular checkpoints along the route, and all competitors are advised to make it to one of these checkpoints to seek help unless utterly incapable of doing so. Mountain rescues are not simple affairs, and for those in trouble the wait could be long.

But despite the variables and dangers associated with the race, the performances of the athletes border on the spectacular. In 2010, Urs Jenzer set a course record, completeing the race in 8 hours, 23 minutes, five seconds. Anita Lehmann holds the women's record, winning in 2010 by more than an hour with a time of 9 hours, 45 minutes.

Bearing in mind the gradients, altitude and the course, these times are impressive for the 80km (50-mile) distance.

As such, the importance of acclimatisation in this environment is vital. Therefore, it is no surprise that the top racers at the Moutainman are local or Alp-based competitors. But for those who don't have the benefit of living somewhere similar, it makes this challenge even tougher and more rewarding to compete. If you do take this one on, though, make sure there are some hills nearby to train on!

Bernard Hug and Anita Lehmann

ATHLETE PERSPECTIVE

Bernard Hug: I had no special mental preparation for the Mountainman. It was the first time I did it, but I knew parts of the course. I always try to have the course – including terrain and next feed stations – in my head as well as possible because I like to be prepared and focus on having a steady performance.

Physically, I did my normal training during the week (I have a full-time job). So I try to run over lunchtime two times a week and once I cycle to work and back (one hour there and an hour-and-a-quarter back). On the weekends I did long training sessions, including hiking with my wife at a slow pace and sometimes races. I always do an overload period of two to three weeks with high training loads, followed by a two-to-three-week taper phase before my main competitions.

Anita Lehman: The mental preparation is done automatically for me. I need not tell myself, 'Now you have to mentally adjust to the race.' I think often in advance of the run, how it will feel and the weather. And I never have bad thoughts, only positive.

I run about three to four times a week, one to one-and-a-half hours. Two times a week I go hiking, six to eight hours. About two to three times a week I go swimming. I have two horses and at least five times a week go riding. I do not have training plans, even a heart rate monitor. I do everything by feel. Always I train haphazardly, but I'm not headless! I'm thinking well, what I do when I train. I do not train so much, but efficiently.

BH: I have knee problems (an inherited predisposition for arthritis). So I have to use massages and keep my stretching up in order to minimise pain. I did a long two-day orienteering race the week prior to the event and the problem I faced was how to recover in six days from running two sessions of five hours in two days.

AL: My head has never been a problem. My head never gives up! It is important to carefully listen to your body and know what it needs. For example, I never really eat anything during a run. But you have to be flexible. If I have a feeling that my body wants something to eat, I eat something. I have no plans and react spontaneously and by feel.

BH: I never really knew at what position I was until five hours into the race. I did not choose the best shoe for this race because it was still wet in the mountains (from the day before) and I chose a shoe that works well only in dry conditions. Therefore I lost a few minutes on the downhills and always had to catch up on the uphills.

I attacked on the beginning of the last climb; until then it was a constant change in the first four positions. I felt good and had no problems with the heat (it was around 30°C/86°F). So I managed to make a good lead and the last 20 minutes were very emotional because I knew I could win it.

AL: The race was very interesting. The woman in second place is better uphill than I, but she had more trouble downhill. At times, she was nearly 15 minutes ahead. But downhill I caught up with her again and again. Because the finish was at the top of the Mount Pilatus, I had in the last downhill passage to get enough of a lead. The last 7km (4 miles) up to Mount Pilatus, I had real paranoia! When I saw that it would be enough for victory, it was a wonderful feeling! What a finish with all the cheering people I had never seen until now! Just gigantic!

Bernard Hug and Anita Lehmann were the 2011 Mountainman winners.

Type Foot
Date September
Distance 246km (152 miles)
Main obstacles Mental
Website www.spartathlon.gr
They call it The world's most gruelling race.

Competitors say
‘It really is a mind-destroying race.’

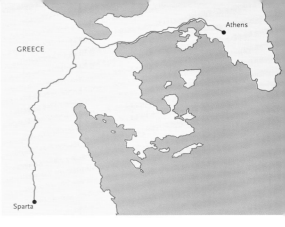

Athens

GREECE

Sparta

Spartathlon

Following in the footsteps of one of the great Greek legends, the Spartathlon sees athletes follow a 250km (155-mile) course across tough, variable terrain against an aggressive time limit.

below A historic race along a historic route

From Odysseus to Hercules, the legends of the Ancient Greeks are packed with tales of truly heroic deeds. But few of these legends have spawned events like the Spartathlon, played out along the same paths and tracks that were trod thousands of years ago. It began at the Battle of Marathon. With Athens under threat from marauding Persian forces, a messenger by the name of Pheidippides was sent to Sparta to ask for reinforcements for the beleaguered Greek forces. According to the account of Herodotus, Pheidippides made the 246km (152-mile) trip from Athens to Sparta by the next day, and a legendary feat of endurance was completed.

And not necessarily repeated for many, many years. That is until John Foden, a retired British RAF Wing Commander – and keen student of ancient Greek history – took four fellow officers to Athens to see whether it was possible to actually cover the distance in a day-and-a-half. On 8 October 1982, the quintet set out. John Scholten was the first to make it to the statue of Leonidas within the timeframe, with Foden close behind. John McCarthy was third across the line, the final finisher after a brutal day-and-a-half of running. The important fact is that they had done it, and the Spartathlon, a now legendary race, was born.

Today, as many as 300 athletes take part in the Spartathlon every year. To qualify for entry an athlete must have either completed a 100km (62-mile) race in less than 10 hours, 30 minutes; completed a 200km (124-mile) race; or competed in the Spartathlon in previous years and reached a predefined checkpoint along the route.

below The cut-offs
are intense

opposite The history
of the race adds to its
allure

Throughout the race there are 75 checkpoints, all of which have cut-off times for runners. And this is perhaps the most challenging aspect of this gruelling race: these cut-offs are aggressively marshalled and anyone failing to make them is removed from the race. As such, every athlete is perpetually conscious of their race against the clock.

Starting at 7 a.m. in the shadows of the Acropolis, the course weaves through the centre of Athens before runners finally hit the 'Sacred Way'. A long-trodden road, athletes follow this path along a series of gradual ascents and descents on the way to Corinth.

Surrounded by landmarks such as the Temple of Apollo and cutting through historic villages and towns, runners soon start to tackle the mountains that separate Ancient Nemea from the sea. Leaving behind the paved roads – and, for many, the last remnants of daylight – the competitors then slowly make their way towards the harder climbs and rougher terrain. With the onset of night, the competitors pass through Lyrkia en route to the base of Mount Sangas. The pathways are more treacherous here, and the combination of night, fatigue (the Mount Base checkpoint marks nearly 160km/100 miles), constant ascent (1200m/3940 feet of climbing) and uncertain terrain often gets the better of even the hardiest athletes.

But for those who make it over the top of Mount Sangas, dawn – and the finish line – awaits. Yes, there might still be more than 100km (62 miles) of running to go and, yes, the night can be long, but perhaps the most taxing part of the race is complete. From Mount Sangas runners head to Tripolis, Tegea (for one final climb) and then the long descent towards Sparta.

And so beneath the shadow of the Statue of Leonidas, thousands of people turn out to greet the athletes that have made it through. All of these spectators are conscious of the supreme physicality of the event. The distance is not the only challenge in the race: athletes have to deal with high temperatures during the day and the cold of night on an exposed mountainside. The terrain is changeable and, at times, unsteady. And the demands of constant exertion against aggressive time limits are immense.

Despite the physical and mental strain the Spartathlon places on competitors, there have been some impressively fast times recorded on the course. The undisputed king of the race is Yiannis Kouros, who holds the four fastest times ever recorded in the race from his four starts (and

four wins). The record he set stands at 20 hours, 25 minutes, a mind-blowing average of over 12km/h (7mph). In 2005, Kouros decided to trace the steps of Pheidippides completely and ran the Athens–Sparta–Athens distance. Sumie Inagaki currently holds the women's record, finishing the women's race in 27 hours, 39 minutes and 49 seconds.

The Greek myths and legends have been retold and reproduced on many stages and in countless books. But the chance to relive the deeds and heroics of some of the greatest figures in history seldom presents itself. The Spartathlon offers athletes the chance to pit themselves against a quite incredible feat of human endurance. Those who complete it know that they have secured themselves a spot in the the pantheon of athletes who have both tackled and completed one of the world's most challenging endurance events.

James Adams

I've been running ultra-marathons for about five years and I first did the Spartathlon in 2009. I found out about it while getting involved in the ultra scene – I've done a lot of the other big races – but among the ultra-running community this is considered a lot more challenging than most. It has a superb history – it is obviously the original race and what we'd be running if the whole marathon story didn't get publicised. I did it a couple of years ago as an event to tick off, and having done it it's become one of those things that I feel like I have to go back to.

What's challenging about the race is that it has cut-offs that are tighter than you would have at any other race. So it's 36 hours, and you have 9½ hours to do the first 80km (50 miles). A lot of the other races will say it's the hottest, or it's the driest, or the wettest, but the Spartathlon is quite simple: it's 246km (153 miles) of road, it's quite warm and hilly but not extreme. But this cut-off makes it difficult. Knowing that the cut-off is there makes people stressed and run in a way that they wouldn't normally, and that's what puts people out of the race: the panic of not making it. You're always looking at your watch, the board and working out how long you've got. It really is a mind-destroying race in that respect.

In other races, even if things go wrong you have enough time to stop and relax – even go to sleep. Whereas with the Spartathlon you just have to keep going.

It's physically very difficult because you're running on the road for 240km (150 miles), and I don't think that anyone could do that without really hurting. There's a mountain climb after 160km (100 miles) and it is quite undulating, and I found that the first time I did it, going down that mountain was really painful. There's no way of doing it without really hurting because it is that kind of race, where you do have to keep moving forwards.

The real key – more so with the Spartathlon than with others – is about staying mentally in control. If you need to pull yourself together in any way, you have to do it on the move. The finish rate is typically around 40 per cent, and that is 40 per cent of people who are actually quite good at running. It's not the kind of race where anyone turns up to try – it's a race where a lot of people put in effort to train themselves up.

James Adams has completed the Spartathlon twice.

AFRICA

Type Foot
Date October
Distance 250km (155 miles)
Main obstacles Heat, terrain
Website www.extrememarathons.com
They call it A challenge – to get past what normal people would regard as crazy and achieve one's personal goals.

Competitors say
If you try and take the desert on and run too hard, it's going to beat you.

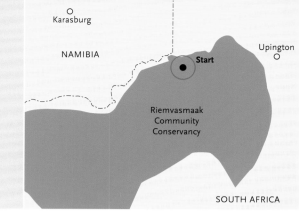

Karasburg

NAMIBIA

Upington

Start

Riemvasmaak
Community
Conservancy

SOUTH AFRICA

Kalahari Augrabies Extreme Marathon

Extremes of temperature, a relentless desert terrain, the presence of some of the most dangerous predators on earth and an unknown course make the 250km (155 miles) of the Kalahari Augrabies Extreme Marathon a true test of human endurance.

right The Kalahari offers a beautiful backdrop to a challenging race

The Kalahari is vast. Stretching 1,500,000 square kilometres (970,000 square miles) through South Africa, Botswana and Namibia, vast seas of red-sand sweep away as far as the eye can see. In this desert, there is little shelter from a relentless sun that raises temperatures to 50°C (122°F) during the day. There are pockets of vegetation and the occasional watering hole, but in this vast wilderness those areas tend to be dominated by the local wildlife and the often uneasy peace between predator and prey.

It is against this backdrop that competitors take on the Kalahari Augrabies Extreme Marathon (KAEM for short): a 250km (155-mile) race through some of the toughest, most spectacular terrain on the planet.

KAEM challenges competitors on a number of levels, and it does so before the race even begins: competitors are unable to plan for the route that lies ahead. In fact, there can be no planning. That is because race organisers change the route every year, revealing it to competitors only on the day of the race briefing – the day before the event actually starts. So while athletes have a rough idea of the kind of terrain they will face over the seven days, nobody actually knows where they are going.

Needless to say, they can rest assured that they will be exposed to the best of the Kalahari. From arid desert to lush vineyards, the course winds its way through the spectacular landscape in stages that range from 30km (18 miles) to 75km (47 miles) in length. Once out on a stage, competitors are responsible for their own welfare. This is a self-sufficient

race, so while water consumption is enforced (and overnight shelter provided) the rest is determined by the needs and wants of the individual.

Meticulous preparation is required along with an understanding of the individual's physical and psychological responses to athletic performance in extremes of temperature. This presents unique challenges for competitors living in cooler climates, who do not necessarily have the ability to become acclimatised to hot weather racing in time for KAEM: they need to manage their body to ensure they make it to the end of each stage. Temperatures along the route can reach in excess of 40°C (104°F), then plummet as low as −5°C (23°F) overnight. As such, it is essential that all athletes fuel and hydrate themselves effectively both during

above The KAEM is a self-sufficient adventure race

and after each stage to ensure that they are in the best possible condition to finish the event. KAEM organisers advise carrying up to 6kg (13lb) of food and drink for the duration of the race, totalling some 21,000 calories for the seven days. The heaviest pack so far recorded on Day One of the KAEM was 16kg (35lb) and included a fillet steak.

But it is out on the course that all of this comes together. While preparation is unquestionably essential, it is the ability to deal with the variables that are thrown at competitors throughout the race that is most important. Because KAEM is a desert race. As such, large sections of the race take place on soft sand or silted riverbeds, making running a challenge. To make matters worse, this sand soaks up the quite considerable heat of the sun, throwing it back at the athletes as they attempt to pass. And on the

days when the wind doesn't blow, it can make the desert feel like hell on earth.

Away from the sand, rocks and boulders line the route, and competitors frequently have to negotiate uneven terrain. The demands of this on a fresh body and mind are hard enough, but on a tired body and heat-ravaged mind they can be brutal, to say the least.

Of course, sand isn't just hard to run on, it gets everywhere too. Sand particles that slip into the socks can rub against sweaty skin to create blisters. Lots of blisters. Competitors in KAEM are warned about the potential for blisters from the outset, and the medical staff who deal with a range of injuries and ailments cite them as the most common complaint. What's more, when out on the course it isn't easy to sit down in the shade and give the feet a break. Of course, shrubbery and the occasional tree line the route. But in the desert the flora can be just as vicious as the fauna, the snakes and ticks (not to mention the big cats) that are known to frequent the area. Athletes have to be as wary of the spikes on the bushes as what lurks beneath the rocks, and all of this can test the mental and physical strength of even the most hardened athlete.

Competitors in the KAEM push their bodies to the limits. They do it in a tough, unforgiving environment. But it is also an environment that rewards persistence, and offers participants the chance to see and do something truly unique. Like so many challenges in this book, KAEM presents a balance between risk and reward, and one that coaxes some of the best athletes on the planet to tackle this majestic wilderness.

right The scenery is truly special

Edward Chapman

Preparing for KAEM is not too much of an issue as long as you're fit. One, you need to be marathon fit. And two, you need to be able to go beyond a marathon as you have a stage of 72–80km (45–50 miles).

The other thing you need to do is a lot of speed work because in the heat your body is going to be working harder. Doing speed work gets your body used to performing at a higher level. Say you're running a 9-minute mile in the UK; the same speed in the desert is going to feel a lot harder. So you have to get your body used to the punishment. And the heat. But being cold and miserable is pretty close to being hot and miserable. Miserable is the same!

The heat does make the race difficult, and the moisture in the air makes it feel hotter. Sometimes when you get 45–47°C (113–116°F) heat and it's bouncing off the rocks, it feels really hot.

The very first time I did it, it was very hot and I was in a really tough ravine. I got too hot, and I didn't drink enough and was sick. And I thought, 'I've come all of this way and I'm going to pull out on the first day.' I crawled into a bit of shade and thought, 'What the hell am I doing?' And then I thought, 'Pull yourself together and get on

with it.' I put down a couple of Dioralyte drinks, sat down for a while, got my temperature down and got on. I was always on the back foot that year. And it taught me never to actually be in that position because you're always going backwards after that. If you can make sure that sort of thing doesn't happen, you're always in control.

The terrain in the Kalahari is difficult. You go through a lot of sand dunes and riverbeds and you're also climbing a lot, which can be challenging. The key is not to try and take the desert on. You've got to manage it and not go beyond that point. If you try and take it on and run too hard, it's going to beat you.

But it's the same for everyone. The atmosphere is competitive but also very friendly. It's like a big family. You know what everyone is going through and everyone else knows what you are going through. And then you're on your own in the desert. It's a nice friendly, warm and supportive atmosphere.

Edward Chapman has competed in numerous ultra-distance races throughout the world. You can find out more about him at edandphil.co.uk.

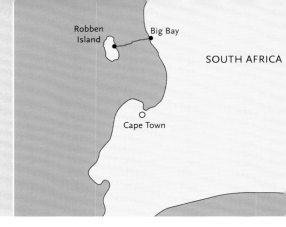

Robben
Island

Big Bay

SOUTH AFRICA

Cape Town

KEY FACTS

Type Swim
Date May
Distance 7.5km (4.6 miles)
Main obstacles Cold, currents
Website www.freedomswim.co.za
They call it One of the toughest, most extreme long-distance cold-water sea swim races in the world.

Competitors say
❝I don't think about the cold or anything like that, the sharks are the main problem for me.❞

Cadiz Freedom Swim

Water that leaves many of its competitors clinically hypothermic, unpredictable currents fuelling some massive swells and some of the most aggressive sharks on the planet make the Cadiz Freedom Swim not only a bona fide endurance challenge, but a scary one too!

below So close, but so far (and with a lot to deal with in the way)

For decades, Robben Island was synonymous with one person: Nelson Mandela. Imprisoned for his beliefs, Mandela struggled against apartheid for 27 years, finally gaining his freedom on 11 February 1990. Three years later, on 27 April 1994, he was elected President of the Rainbow Nation. The Cadiz Freedom Swim, which takes place on or around that date is, in part, a celebration of Mandela's release and the end of apartheid in South Africa.

It is also one of the world's toughest swimming races. From its inception in 2001, the Cadiz Freedom Swim has grown in both popularity and stature year on year. These days the field has swollen to more than 400 competitors, and the race often attracts some of the best long-distance swimmers in the world. They all come with one singular purpose: to conquer the 7.5km (4.6-mile) strait that separated the inmates of Robben Island from the Cape Town mainland.

AFRICA
64

But it isn't easy. Because as well as the sheer physical demands of racing in open, tidal water, the Cadiz Freedom Swim throws in a series of additional factors to challenge participants.

First off, there is the water itself. The race takes place towards the end of April or the beginning of May every year. Despite coming off the back of the South African summer, the water temperature ranges from 9 to 14°C (48–57°F). A significant period of constant immersion in water this cold places an incredible strain on the body. Legs and arms fatigue faster in cold water, as the body moves the blood to the core to protect the organs. What's more, the Cadiz Freedom Swim is a non-wetsuit swim, meaning that competitors can wear nothing more than a swimsuit, goggles and a swim cap. As a result, it is not uncommon for athletes to emerge from the water with a core temperature as low as 30°C (86°F) – medically on the borderlines of hypothermia. Of course, organisers provide medical tents and equipment to ensure that any competitor suffering from the affects of prolonged immersion in cold water is cared for. The risks and the challenges, however, are very real.

But the temperature of the water is just one facet of an incredibly challenging race. Add to the water temperature the currents and swells that batter the strait between Robben Island and the mainland, and you begin to gain an understanding of why the race deserves a place in this book.

above Competitors line up at the start of a tough couple of hours

left Out into the swells and waters famous for their dense population of great white sharks

above Real
competitors do
it in trunks

Swells as large as 4m (13 feet) run through the strait, and the currents that churn the water between Robben Island and the mainland are notoriously fierce. Indeed, it is not uncommon for support boats to struggle in the water, let alone the swimmers themselves.

And then there are the sharks. Love them or hate them, one thing that South Africa is famous for is its concentration of great white sharks. There is no legislating for these animals during the race, and usually the presence of so many people and boats in one area negates such a threat. But swimming in shark-infested waters can play heavily on the minds of the competitors – particularly those not used to competing in such conditions. As with any long-distance race, psychology is key to completing the event, and the fact that something might be eyeing you up for lunch can undoubtedly disrupt a competitor's focus.

Because of these factors, the race is not just open to anyone. Competitors have to qualify by having completed the swim solo (and had this recognised), having completed a 5km (3-mile) cold-water swim or having finished one of the qualifying swims outlined by the organisers. These stipulations are put in place to ensure that when the heart starts pumping and the feet touch the water, the body doesn't go into terminal shutdown.

Once the race begins, swimmers must have their own support crew. Every solo swimmer and each relay team must be accompanied by a motorised boat, but that boat cannot provide any assistance to the swimmer in any way. Elite swimmers can apply to be accompanied by a paddler instead of the motorised boat, but whether or not they can do so is down to the organising committee.

The competition itself is fierce. Some of the best open-water swimmers in the world regularly take on the challenge of Cadiz, battling it out for the US$10,000 prize. Christof Wandrastch – a one-time holder of the record for crossing the English Channel – holds the current course record for the Cadiz Freedom Swim (1 hour, 33 minutes and 11 seconds), while Olympian and Paralympic gold medallist Nathalie Du Toit currently holds the women's record with 1 hour, 35 minutes.

The Cadiz Freedom Swim is a true test of human endurance. Demanding competitors face up to physical, physiological and psychological challenges every stroke of the way, it offers them no place to hide once they enter the water. For those who conquer the challenge, there is a well-earned beanie, a T-shirt and a medal waiting at the other end (and probably a hot cup of tea).

below The cold starts here

Petar Stoychev

I got into marathon swimming because I wanted to travel around the world and see different places. After I started, I slowly became one of the best in the world and that gave me motivation to continue. The feeling and the emotion of being number one cannot compare to anything else. To be number one at anything and the feeling that you are number one is great. But every day is hard work. On average, I swim between 70 and 90km (44–56 miles) per week – when I was younger, I swam more.

I am very strong mentally. All these years when I was training with partners I taught myself to win all the training sessions. Then that happens in the competitions. Just having the feeling that you need to win every event. That slowly becomes part of your life and then you want to be a winner for all of your life.

I don't like to swim in cold water in training, which made preparing for the Cadiz Freedom Swim more difficult. I only like to race in these conditions. The cold makes the body feel very slow and the muscles don't feel good in the water. It is more difficult to get good results after this kind of training – it is harder to give 100 per cent in the race.

Mental preparation is always very important for the Freedom Swim. I wanted to participate and win that race because it was important for me to show myself that I am good enough in 11–12°C (51–53°F) water. Also, I'm really scared of the sharks. It always plays on my mind. I don't think about the cold or anything like that; the sharks are the main problem for me. And I hope that next year, if they invite me, I will be able to have a shark shield.

Sometimes during the race you have tough moments: you can't move your arms or you don't have the power to push your arms to accelerate. But this all depends on the training and the conditioning of your body. Sometimes the water temperature can affect you as well. But everything is in your mind and you just have to keep on pushing.

Petar Stoychev was the first person to swim the English Channel in under seven hours (6 hours, 57 minutes and 50 seconds). He won the 2011 Cadiz Freedom Swim in 1 hour, 51 minutes and 54 seconds. For more information, visit petarstoychev.com

ATHLETE PERSPECTIVE

Type Bike | **Date** March/April
Distance Variable (up to 900km/560 miles)
Main obstacles Distance, technical, elevation
    change, terrain
Website www.cape-epic.com
They call it The magical and untamed African
    Mountain Bike Race.

Competitors say
❝While you wrestle your bike across its vast and rugged beauty, Africa is putting on a show all around you.❞

Cape Epic

An always changing course that couples the demand for technical skill with outstanding levels of fitness, the Cape Epic takes riders on a challenging race through some of South Africa's most stunning – and rarely seen – terrain.

above Drafting is allowed

One good idea can often spawn many more. That is the case with the Cape Epic, a mountain bike race conceived on the beaches of Costa Rica following Kevin Vermaak's successful completion of La Ruta de Los Conquistadores. Vermaak looked at La Ruta, one of the toughest mountain bike races on the planet, and wondered if it was possible to showcase the best of South Africa in a similar stage race.

He worked out that it was. Heading home in 2004, Vermaak started preparations for the inaugural Cape Epic – a point-to-point race from the East to the West Cape of South Africa.

The route might be different now – in fact, it is different every year – but the ethos behind the Cape Epic remains the same: to show off the 'untamed' Africa. And that is why the organisers have put in place a number of rules. Every rider has to be part of a team of two. Every team must remain within two minutes of one another at all times (this is regulated by timing mats, and three infractions leads to a disqualification) and the time of the second rider across the line is the one that is recorded. In that respect, the Cape Epic is unique.

Although there are plenty of team events in various ultra-distance races around the world, there are few that use technology to enforce the rules. If, for any reason, a team member has to retire from the race, then riders can compete individually as 'outcasts' (they get a special jersey), but they are no longer part of the race and cannot interfere or offer help to any athletes still competing.

The rules are strictly enforced, but they are there for a reason. The Cape Epic takes riders through extreme, challenging environments with little help or assistance for miles around. And as a largely self-supported event, the competitors need to work as a team to ensure the successful completion of single stages, let alone the entire race.

Taking place over eight stages, the full distance of the race has varied every year since it began, from 685km (425 miles) in 2009 (the shortest race) to 966km (600 miles) in 2008 (the longest). But it is not just the length of the race that tests the athletes, but the brutality of the climbs involved. Taking in plenty of hilly – often mountainous – terrain, competitors can expect to face anything up to 16,000m (52,500 feet) of climbing – almost twice the height of Mount Everest – over the course of the event.

The sheer volume of vertical metres climbed, coupled with the severity of the gradients and the terrain on which the climbs take place (anything from concrete paths through to sand), requires not only supreme strength but also excellent bike-handling skills. But it is perhaps the descents in this race that challenge riders the most. These descents, which frequently force riders to tackle uneven terrain such as loose rocks or sand, are often down perilously steep tracks on exposed routes.

This is technical, high-risk riding, and competitors cannot afford to make a serious error. And that can easily occur, given the spectacular nature of the surroundings and the human variable of slower reaction times as heat and general fatigue take their toll. As anyone who has ever raced mountain bikes can attest, that can destroy your chances of completing the race.

So too can a lack of mechanical awareness. The scarcity of help along the route means that all riders need to be able to prepare and repair their own bikes during the course of the event. The organisers do offer bike servicing during the course of the race, but once riders are out on the trail it is up to them.

Of course, no race through the South African wilderness would be complete without a mention of the wildlife that can

below Teams of two must compete and complete together

impact the athletes. Thorns lining the route are a constant risk not only to riders but also to their tyres; stinging flies, snakes, spiders, animals that might want to eat you ... And though their actual threat may be limited, psychology is key in every ultra-distance race, and every rider knows that these creatures are out there.

But they are some of the elements that make the event so special. The Cape Epic rewards those who attempt to take her on. The scenery is spectacular, the routes traverse vast areas of private land that few cyclists – few people, for that matter – get to see, and it is a true journey into the remote heart of an incredible country.

Yes, the Cape Epic really does have it all. It pushes participants harder, further and up more mountains than most races in the world; it brings out the best in their physical and technical skills; and it brings them face to face with some of the most spectacular and challenging scenery on earth. In short, it is truly an epic event.

above Challenging terrain is a standout for the Cape Epic

Nic Lamond

The Absa Cape Epic is not about winning; it is about connection. There's a primal connection to the unforgiving African earth you traverse. You feel deeply connected, even indebted, to fellow competitors, often bound by hardship and courage and triumph at the end of each day. And, of course, you feel connected to your bike, whose wheels carry your dreams and expectations.

Whether you're a world champion, one of the planet's elite cyclists, or part of the large majority of amateur adventurers, the same thing awaits every Absa Cape Epic entrant: a lifetime of emotion stuffed into eight glorious days. Finishing the Absa Cape Epic comes down to three things: your bike, your body and your buddy. Look after these three things, ensure that they arrive intact at the end of each of the gruelling eight days, and the race is yours.

Of course, it's not quite that simple. There's plenty of work involved in making sure your Cape Epic experience has the best chance of success. And the beauty is that it's no different for the pros. Months of research goes into setting up your bike and understanding all the gear that goes with off-road endurance racing. Hours in the saddle and the gym get you close to as fit as you'll ever be in your life. And if he or she isn't already, your riding buddy will become the closest relationship you've ever forged.

If you get all these things right, well, you've got a chance. That's right; prepare every detail months in advance, and there are still no guarantees. A fourth piece of the Epic puzzle needs to fall in place: luck. The race can be a cruel master and luck, or the lack of it, can dash the dreams you've been building over months in a matter of seconds.

The thrill of negotiating tricky, tight descents and long, loose climbs can be overwhelming. While you wrestle your bike across its vast and rugged beauty, Africa is putting on a show all around you. It is an exhilarating reward for eight full days, yet through the myriad distractions of getting to the finish line you have to constantly remind yourself to feel the connections around you and drink it all in. This is why you are here.

Nic Lamond has completed the Cape Epic six times.

Type Bike
Date October
Distance 12,000km (7500 miles)
Main obstacles Distance, terrain, weather
Website www.tourdafrique.com
They call it A test of mind, body and bike.

Competitors say
‘The tour was one of the defining events of my life, because it gave me insight into who I am, what I value and what I can accomplish. The tour's rewards, ultimately, are much, much bigger than its challenges.’

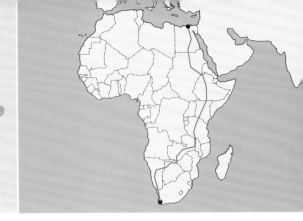

Tour d'Afrique

An epic adventure dissecting the heart of one of the most fascinating continents on the planet, the Tour d'Afrique not only challenges competitors' resolve, it opens their eyes and minds to a different world.

below Africa's wildlife adds further excitement

The Tour d'Afrique is unlike many of the challenges profiled in this book. At its heart, it is a tour. A grand tour, but a tour nevertheless. From the shadows of the Pyramids to the crashing seas of Cape Town, it is a journey through the heart of one of the world's most vibrant – and untouched – continents. But it would be wrong to describe the Tour d'Afrique as simply a sightseeing jolly. Within the Tour there is a race, and that race is as demanding – and long – as any of the challenges listed within these pages.

Covering over 12,000km (7500 miles), the race of the Tour d'Afrique is divided into 94 stages and eight major sections. This allows those who cannot commit to spending four months traversing the length of Africa to join at least part of the race (although, of course, they do not figure in the overall classifications). During the course of the race, competitors can expect to tackle 69 full race days, four individual time trials and eight half-race days (typically reduced due to border crossings or proximity to cities). To cover the distance in the allotted time, the average stage length is 123km (77 miles) and most range from 80km (50 miles) to 200km (125 miles).

All of this is on a mountain bike, and a lot of this is on unpaved roads. That is a challenging itinerary, to say the least. To legislate for physical or mechanical issues, competitors are permitted a certain amount of 'grace' days. This means that all athletes can scratch their worst stage times from their overall time, but on some particularly tough stages these rules do not apply. Of course, the athlete with the lowest accumulated time at the conclusion of the race is the winner.

But to get to that stage, there is a lot of cycling to do. Starting out in the shadows of the pyramids, some 400 competitors cycle through Egypt to the Red Sea before joining the Nile at Qena. From there, a quick overnight ferry deposits the racers on the edge of 'real' Africa: Sudan. From this point onwards, the race begins to pierce the heart of a truly fascinating continent. The River Nile accompanies the race as far as Khartoum, and Section One (of Eight) is complete at 1955km (1214 miles).

below The stunning
scenery often presents
a welcome distraction

opposite There
aren't many more
spectacular start lines
in sport

As Stage Two begins, so do some of the more taxing
challenges. While the journey from Sudan to Ethiopia is
spectacular, the challenges are real. Not only is the fatigue
beginning to set in (if it hasn't already), but the elevation gain
means cyclists can expect to climb as much as 2500m (8200
feet) in a single day. As such, the technical and physical
demands of the race at this stage are immense. Competitors
are not only dealing with cumulative fatigue from numerous
days in the saddle, but the challenge of cycling at altitude is
great. As, for that matter, is the challenge of cycling in the
heat of one of the driest countries on the planet.

The desert doesn't last long, though. Soon rock
becomes field, and the lush countryside of Kenya takes
over. For the most part, the riding here is easier, on at least
semi-paved roads. But towards the end of the Kenyan leg,
riders face six taxing days crossing the unpaved volcanic
'fields' of the Dida Galgalu desert.

So the journey continues. Kenya, Tanzania, Malawi,
Zambia (and the Victoria Falls), Namibia and finally South
Africa, the Tour d'Afrique is an epic journey through some
incredible landscape. On the way competitors are almost
guaranteed to see lions, elephants, giraffes, wildebeest,
crocodiles ... the list is endless.

But just as the beauty and splendour of the Tour is
obvious, so is the brutal nature of the race. Of course,
competitors are supported along the way by the tour
organisers. But only the athlete can deal with the long days of
rugged riding through a tough environment. The cumulative
fatigue from an event like this is massive, and competitors
have to be sure to manage their nutrition, hydration and
recovery effectively to stand a chance of being classified at
the end of each section, let alone the race. And while the
local wildlife may be spectacular, it is not without its risks.

Then, of course, there is the political volatility of the
continent. While the route is set, organisers are always
conscious of the need to change direction should politics

present a threat to competitors, as happened in 2003 when the race avoided Kenya. But for the most part, these incidences are rare.

Records for crossing Africa by bike have been set twice in the Tour, in 2003 and 2010. These have subsequently been revised in a non-tour ride, by Dutchman Robert Knol, who covered the distance in an incredible 70-day journey at an average of just under 22km/h (13mph).

An adventure, a challenge and a once-in-a-lifetime experience, the Tour d'Afrique is an epic race through the heart of one of the most fascinating continents on the planet. Only the strongest, most resilient cyclists can expect to complete the distance, but those who do, know they have achieved something very special.

left As can be expected when traversing a continent, the weather can be mixed

David Houghton

I prepared for the event by doing a lot of riding. I'd completed a 7500km (4660-mile) ride across Canada the previous year, and I competed in various rides and races to keep the mileage up. To prepare mentally is much more difficult. The best that I could do was to know that I had everything I needed for my own safety and comfort; that my bike was as prepared as it could be; and that I'd need to dig down into my reserves of patience and strength to complete the Tour.

It's impossible to replicate the conditions: the heat, the nasty road surfaces, and the sheer exhaustion of riding day after day after day. I did a lot of riding – on the bike, on the trainer and in spinning classes – but that could only do so much to prepare my body for the endurance that was necessary. The good thing is that the smooth roads of Egypt provide a good warm-up for the more substantial challenges of Sudan, Ethiopia and Kenya.

It became clear very early on that I wasn't going to win the race. So I focused on just finishing every day, no matter how long it took. Luckily, every day provided some diversion that helped take my mind off the challenges, at least momentarily. It might be kids I met in a village along the way, a warm Coke, or a beautiful, stark African landscape. I tried to keep all my senses as receptive as possible and not crawl into self-pity.

The list of physical issues is different for every rider. For me, it included saddle sores, dehydration, three weeks of diarrhoea and a crash in Tanzania that required stitches. Mentally, every rider suffers through the same issues: fatigue, doubt and the kind of soul-searching that comes after months of challenge. Every rider finds their own way of dealing with these issues and has to resolve them on their own terms.

Finishing the tour was an incredible feeling. I cried as we cycled into Cape Town, out of joy and relief and gratitude. The Tour provided me with four months that I remember with incredible clarity; I can recall the detail of every day. The Tour was one of the defining events of my life, because it gave me insight into who I am, what I value and what I can accomplish. The Tour's rewards, ultimately, are much, much bigger than its challenges.

David Houghton is an ultra-distance cyclist who competed in the 2005 Tour d'Afrique and has previously cycled 7500km (4660 miles) across Canada.

Type Foot
Date May/June
Distance 89km (55 miles)
Main obstacles Elevation change
Website www.comrades.com
They call it Celebrating the triumph of mankind's spirit over adversity.

Competitors say
'Whether it's an uphill or downhill year, you always prefer the one you are not doing.'

Comrades Marathon

Uphill one year, downhill the next, the Comrades Marathon is not only the world's oldest and largest ultra, but also the most famous. And while the terrain of the Comrades may not make it the toughest ultra-marathon in the world, the challenges that athletes face on the unforgiving course give it a legendary status in the endurance community.

below The Comrades is one of the world's largest ultras

right Quality athletes compete in the race each year

Unlike most other races outlined in this book, the Comrades Marathon has a history steeped in war. When Vic Clapham returned from World War I, he decided that he wanted to remember – and honour – the men that he had fought alongside in a unique way. Thinking back to the 2735km (1700 miles) of marching that he had undertaken through the eastern savannahs of Africa during the war, Vic settled

on the idea of launching a marathon. At first reluctant, the authorities eventually granted a licence to run the Comrades Marathon on 24 May 1921. Just 34 runners started the race that day, and only 16 of them finished. It was won by Bill Rowan in 8 hours, 59 minutes – the slowest winning time in the history of the race. Since then, the Comrades Marathon has been run every year – except during the years of World War II (1939–45).

And the numbers participating in the race have grown accordingly. At the start of the 2012 race, 18,000 heard Max Trimborn's impersonation of a cock's crow to start the race (a long-standing Comrades tradition). And while many of these went much faster than Rowan's 1921 winning time, the challenges that faced them remained identical.

Although run in the early South African winter, the race can be subjected to extreme weather conditions, with average

daytime temperatures falling as low as 3°C (37°F) and reaching as high as 30°C (86°F). But the weather is much less a factor than the course itself.

Run 'down' on odd years and 'up' on even years, the race takes in 89km (55 miles) of tarmac roads from Pietermaritzburg to Durban (or vice versa) in the state of KwaZulu-Natal. That's not to say that the downhill run is one long, continuous descent. Along the way, athletes are forced to tackle the Big Five – Cowie's Hill, Field's Hill, Botha's Hill, Inchanga and Polly Shortts – a series of hills that test the mettle of every athlete. This repeated elevation change is enough to get the lactic acid burning in the leg muscles.

Physically, both ascending and descending on the run is not easy. To an armchair athlete, the downhill run might seem easier. However, the pressure that constant descent puts on your quads and knees is immense, not to mention the change in stride length that can lead to physical stress. Needless to say, uphill is no easier. Despite promoting better running form (shorter stride patterns and a lean-in), the simple muscle sapping effort it takes to climb continuously on an undulating course from sea level to the highest point (870m/2855 feet above sea level) pushes athletes to their limits.

This explains why in 2003 they raised the cut-off time from 11 to 12 hours. All entrants must have met qualifying standards within a specified time frame, ensuring that no marathon novices attempt to take on the challenge. Once out on the course, there are various cut-off times ahead

below Up one year, down the next, each race presents unique challenges

of the 12-hour race finish. For those who do make it to the top or bottom of the hill(s), there are medals based on their position and/or race time (gold for the first 10 men and women across the line to copper for anyone finishing between 11 and 12 hours), and there are colour-coded race numbers to identify the number of race finishes.

Steeped in history and tradition, the Comrades Marathon requires all those who take up her gauntlet to search deep for their inner reserves. With alternating directions – both presenting their own challenges – it offers a true test of human endurance in the largest ultra-marathon field on earth.

left A 12-hour cut-off time ensures a quality field of athletes

Bruce **Fordyce**

Preparing for Comrades is not that different from training for a normal marathon. The training was very similar except that I would throw in a few longer runs – that would be anything from marathon distance maybe up to about 64km (40 miles) or so.

Whether it's an uphill or downhill year, you always prefer the one you are not doing. I mean, is there such a thing as an easier one? The 'down' run is a little bit faster. If anyone is going for a specific medal and you are a borderline case, then it is better to go for the 'down' run. Although you have to remember that, while it may be quicker, it also hurts more. You do a lot of the downhill running in the last part of the race. Until you get to that point, most of it resembles the 'up' run in that it is just rolling hills and quite a few uphills, downhills and flat stuff. Then it plummets down to the coast at a point where your legs are very tired and they've taken a lot and then you've got to go downhill. So it does cause quite a lot of muscle damage and it's a sore run.

Probably the toughest part of the 'down' run is at 20km (12 miles) to go, when you reach a place called Pine Town. It's dry and muggy because you are starting to pick up the Durban atmosphere. It's noisy and it's quite a dull place and you have to dig deep.

But the 'up' run is a tough run because it seems for the first half that all you do is climb. You just go up and up and up. It gets particularly tough at a place called Harrison Flats. You've got about 30km (18 miles) to go and it is flat and hot and dry and dusty. The surroundings are dull, and there's not a lot of spectator support. At the end of that flat bit, you reach some of the famous big hills of the 'up' run. Polly Shortts is the monster hill that you hit when you have 8km (5 miles) to go – it's a killer hill that breaks a lot of people.

I'm very proud of the races I've had, but also have had some that I could have done better in. What all of us learn is that it is easier to keep on going than to drop out. If you drop out, you have to live with yourself for the following 365 days and redeem yourself in another run.

Comrades is very special. In the course of one day, you can experience living a whole lifetime. It is such an emotional, physical, spiritual ... everything to experience the challenge of that race.

Bruce Fordyce has won the Comrades Marathon a record nine times (including eight in a row). He has completed the race 29 times.

KEY FACTS

Type Canoe
Date February
Distance 125km (78 miles)
Main obstacles Technical
Website www.dusi.co.za
They call it Africa's premier canoe challenge.

Competitors say
❛There is no better feeling than after a great race to paddle in past the crowds to loud cheers, all of a sudden making every bit of pain you have experienced over the past three days very worthwhile!❜

SOUTH AFRICA

Start
Pietermaritzburg

Finish
Durban O

Dusi Canoe Marathon

A fearsome river that cuts through a challenging environment. Whether competitors in the Dusi Canoe Marathon choose to go by water or land, the challenges they face are extreme.

below The challenges en route are frequent and exhausting

Thousands of miles from home, with World War II raging all around him, Ian Player had a thought. Gazing into a campfire, he wondered whether it was possible to paddle a canoe from Pietermaritzburg to Durban. At the time, it must have seemed like little more than a flight of fancy. Little did Player know that his idea was the start of one of the greatest canoe races on the African continent.

Returning from the war, Player put thoughts into action. An initial attempt at the Dusi failed at the midway point. But on 22 December 1950 Player was joined by seven other paddlers in an attempt to conquer the infamous stretch of river. Six days, 8 hours and 15 minutes later, he became the first man to 'do the Dusi'. Player had overcome treacherous conditions, flash flooding and a snake bite en route to the finish, but he had proved that it could be done. And as is so often the case with challenges of this nature, once Player had done it, others soon followed. Within five years, more than 40 paddlers were tackling the Dusi, and 50 years later the field has swollen to more than 2000.

What attracts competitors to tackle this exhausting – and, at times, downright dangerous – challenge? Just that: the challenge. Because while the time it takes to do the Dusi has dropped considerably (the current record stands at a mere eight hours), the challenges remain the same. When Player first attempted the course, he did it in one long effort. Today – and for many years now – competitors are forced to paddle the Dusi over three days with two overnight stops. The three days are broken down into stages of 45km (28 miles), 45km (28 miles)

and 35km (22 miles). And each stage presents challenges for the competitors, pros and amateurs alike.

Those challenges begin immediately. Day One pits athletes against their first water 'obstacle': Ernie Pearce Weir. Far from the most challenging part of the course, it is a solid introduction to the challenges that lie ahead as paddlers queue up to tackle the chute through the middle of the weir one by one. Then the fun begins. Weirs are commonplace, as are white water rapids that range from Grade Two (pretty average) to Grade Four (hard). What's more, on every stage – and usually on multiple occasions – competitors have to portage their kayak for anything up to 5km (3 miles) at a time.

As competitors make their way along the Dusi, the severity of rapids, the length of the portages and the challenges of the weirs simply increase. As does the fatigue. Multiple days of constant paddling through the hottest month of the year place a huge mental and physical strain on the competitors. And when tired arms, aching backs and weary minds take on Grade 4 rapids, the possibility for errors and resultant injuries increase exponentially. Of course, when facing rapids like the Island or the Washing Machine, less-than-confident competitors have the option to portage their kayak. But for those who don't, the advice generally ranges from 'good luck' to 'hang on'. Sections of the Dusi are fast and furious, and only the most competent kayakers are advised to tackle them.

above Portaging is an option on the toughest rapids

But while portaging may be the safest option, it is not the physically easiest. The constant strain of getting in and out of a kayak, transporting the boat and any equipment needed for the race, as well as negotiating uneven, occasionally tricky pathways, makes this option less than ideal. What's more, the environment that competitors have to portage their boats through can cause problems. Snakes are commonplace, as are ticks, and anyone who has spent time either racing or spectating is advised to be checked for bilharzia and rickettsia (both survivable but occasionally fatal).

Of course, it goes without saying that there is one element of the Dusi Canoe Marathon which is essential – and which can be deadly: the river. In 2011, organisers changed the date of the race from December to February because of problems associated with low river levels. The change made conditions much better, but water quality is a constant battle that the organisers face. Low water levels mean more exposed rocks and so the greater the opportunity for damaged boats and people. It also means more portaging.

The rules around the Dusi River Marathon are pretty strict. Competitors have a choice of class to enter: K1, K2,

White Water, Touring or Touring Canadian classes. K1 and K2 are considered the 'main' classes, with the designate of 'main class' alternating between the two categories each year. Paddlers who choose it can be 'seconded' (have a support team), with only the designated second allowed to assist competitors during the race.

Needless to say, a race like the Dusi has its fair share of legends and records. Undoubtedly, the legend of legends in the race is the late Graeme Pope-Ellis, or 'the Dusi King', who completed the Dusi Canoe Marathon a record 46 times. The course record, meanwhile, stands at an incredible 8 hours, 3 minutes in the K1 class, a testament to the skill and strength of some of the pros who tackle the race.

While the structure of the Dusi Canoe Marathon has changed, the route and the challenges of the race are very much the same. It is a race that forces competitors to tackle not only severe river conditions, but also face up to the mental and physical challenges that line the route. But in doing so, they not only tackle one of the toughest canoe races on the planet, but can claim to be one of the few to 'do the Dusi'.

Ant Stott

ATHLETE PERSPECTIVE

Preparing for the Dusi both mentally and physically starts many months before the race. With the Dusi being such a unique race you need to be well prepared in both the paddling and running departments. With there being so many rapids and varying water levels, one needs to spend a lot of time in the valley learning the different lines and portage options for each different water level. For a race like this, being purely running fit is not enough. Many hours need to be spent running with your kayak on goat and cattle paths. The hills in the race are very challenging, so it is worthwhile throwing in some very big hill or mountain running sessions into the programme.

Once you have done all of the hard training, you will be mentally prepared because you now know what your body is capable of doing!

Running with a kayak for such great distances is not normal and you have to do your best to avoid strange running injuries. Your boat is weighed in dry at a minimum of 12kg (26lb). Wet, it is around 13kg (29lb); paddle and foot pump, 1kg (2.2lb); wet shoes, spray deck, clothes and life jacket about 1.5kg (3lb); juice 2kg (4.5lb). You are looking at a running total of about 18kg (40lb). On Day One you are running about 16km (10 miles), so preparing for this type of running is a huge challenge. Being able to spend time on the river is hugely important, but when there is no rain for weeks at a time, then there is no water to paddle on!

I always try to do training sessions that are a lot harder than the race itself. This means that by the time you get to the race you have already put your body through much worse, making the race more manageable. The faster you get to the finish of each stage, the more time you get to rest for the next one! The juice we race with is vital, and drinking provides us with everything we need to keep going in the heat at high intensity.

Being a fairly tricky river coupled with gruelling portages, there is a lot that can go wrong. Your equipment should be checked over and over again before each stage, to avoid any mechanical problems during the race. Broken boats as a result of smashing into rocks are very common. Some people break their boats in two pieces but then put them back together again with sticks, duct tape and/or fibreglass in order to continue. Sprained ankles are strapped and the competitors soldier on. Cuts are also taped up and stitched at the overnight stops.

Once you cross that finish line in Durban, every single paddler feels like they have achieved something huge. There is no better feeling than after a great race to paddle in past the crowds to loud cheers, all of a sudden making every bit of pain you have experienced over the past three days very worthwhile! Strangely, when you wake up on the Sunday after the race, your body feels better than it did the day before. This in itself is enough to make you want to start preparing for the following year's race almost immediately.

Ant Stott was the 2008 World K2 Marathon Champion. For more information, visit antstott.wordpress.com

Type Foot
Date April
Distance 240km (150 miles)
Main obstacles Heat
Website www.darbaroud.com
They call it A six-day marathon across the Sahara Desert.

Competitors say
6 *Some 240km (150 miles) across one of the greatest deserts in the world, the Marathon des Sables has gained worldwide attention for the physicality of the event and the conditions those who complete it have to conquer.* 9

Start
Erfoud
MOROCCO
Tazzarine
Finish

Marathon des Sables

The Sahara is the second largest desert on the planet. Covering most of Northern Africa, this mighty sandpit is almost equal in size to Europe or North America. But unlike these two great continents, the Sahara isn't full of jostling cities or diverse ecospheres. Instead it is dry, stark and stunning. Sand dunes reach up to 180m (590 feet) into the deep blue sky. The wind shapes and moulds them as it whips through the desert, creating natural obstacles for the few living creatures in the desert to pass. And for the competitors in the Marathon Des Sables to tackle.

below The leading runners are superb athletes

One of the best-known endurance races on the planet, the Marathon Des Sables (or MDS) is a 240km (150-mile) race across the Sahara Desert, in southern Morocco. Competitors tackle the multi-stage race over as many as six days, although the business end of the field completes the journey in five. Along the way they are expected to tackle stages ranging from 17.5km (11 miles) to 82km (51 miles) in heat that can easily exceed 48°C (120°F).

The challenge is formidable for those who race it, and athletes who tackle it must be in supreme physical condition, if only to deal with the demands of completing the equivalent of more than five marathons in just six days. What's more,

huge sections of the MDS take place on soft, unforgiving sand. Running on this kind of sand is not only exhausting but very difficult to prepare for. It can also be debilitating for the feet. The combination of fine sand particles and the hot weather is a perfect recipe for blisters to develop.

At no point is this more likely than on the notorious 'long' stage, which can range from 80 to 90km (48–57 miles). While the elite who race can, as expected, complete this stage in lightning-quick times, those who are not so adept at desert or ultra-marathon running have been known to finish almost a day later than the fastest athletes. In that instance, competitors are running through the day and night, following a course through a sandy, inhospitable environment.

above An epic race across the world's largest sand desert

The sand can also present a very real threat to athletes. Competitors in the Marathon Des Sables are repeatedly warned about the dangers of sandstorms. When the wind whips through the desert, bringing with it a cloud of sand and dust, it become almost impossible for athletes to determine either the route or direction. In such instances, organisers advise athletes to stay completely still until the storm has passed. In reality, not everyone does and athletes have been known to become lost in the desert after failing to heed safety advice.

The desert is not a place to be lost. As such, the safety of the competitors is of paramount importance for the organisers of the race. Every athlete has to carry with them an extensive list of mandatory items, which range from a distress flare to an anti-venom pump. What's more, all athletes have to provide their own food for the duration of the event; it is transported between stages by the race crew. Regulations demand that each competitor carries an absolute minimum of 2000 calories per day (14,000 calories in total). Water is distributed by the support crew during the race, and every athlete has to carry a certain amount of liquids with them. The added weight of water, food and

emergency equipment places an additional strain on athletes who are already facing multiple long days in the desert. Factoring in the weight of a rucksack (in both training and on race day) is therefore another key preparation.

Competitors can choose to tackle the Marathon Des Sables as individuals or as teams; around 30 per cent take the team option. Needless to say, some of the statistics around the race are impressive. The course changes from year to year, making actual historical comparisons between winners' times difficult. Lahcen Ahansal is a nine-time winner of the race (his brother has won it three times) and the average speed that the winner often runs is close to 14km/h (8.5mph).

These numbers are as impressive as the race itself. A relentless run through the heart of possibly the most famous desert on the planet, the Marathon des Sables forces athletes to face up to one of the most extreme environments on earth. Those who complete the challenge may have conquered only a small part of this great desert, but they join an elite group of individuals who can claim to have conquered the mighty Sahara.

Nick Gracie

When I did the Marathon des Sables, I enjoyed it a lot. It is a great challenge for people to take on – especially if they haven't done a lot of events and ultra-marathons. It's not as tough as some races because every night you get the chance to rest, recover, sort your feet out and then do it again the next day. But it is a great challenge for people, and for me, it was a springboard to other events.

To prepare for it, you need to do a lot of long runs with your backpack. You need to get all of the kit ready that works for you, and then you need to work out how much food you have to carry for that stage because every day you have to carry that much food in your backpack. There's a lot of admin in that respect because you have to work out how many calories you need per day and how you get them.

Getting your feet conditioned is also really important. The reason that most people don't finish that race is because they get blisters. Physically you could just take trekking poles and walk it and finish it. But people's feet do get pretty torn up if they don't take care of them and toughen them up. The only way to do that is to walk on them. Try and walk around barefoot and then just spend a lot of time walking, and make sure you have the perfect shoes.

Most people think they will run the whole thing, so they take a pair of shoes and run in them. But you will spend a lot of time walking, which can be quite different. So you need to wear your shoes in. I found a pair of shoes that fitted well and then bought two pairs exactly the same. I wore one pair the whole time during training and then about three weeks before the race I had this brand new pair of shoes that I wore in a bit – but effectively had new shoes for the event – and they were one size too big (because your feet swell up in the heat). I'm lucky in that I have tough feet, but it is key to prepare them.

The course itself changes every year, but generally you're running on hard-packed sand, which isn't too bad to run on. There are some parts where there is some quite soft sand and dunes and that are quite hard work. It's relatively hot – not crazy hot – and it's a dry heat, which is much easier to deal with than humid races. So the conditions are not impossible. You just need to make sure you have the right clothing and equipment. But the terrain is sand dunes and deserts. It is challenging. The people that do it these days find it a really good challenge. If you're used to running marathons, then it is a definite step up.

Nick Gracie has completed numerous ultra-distance events around the world. A former Adventure Racing world champion, Nick is a member of the Adidas Terrex team.

ASIA

Type Foot
Date May
Distance 26.4 miles (42.2km)
Main obstacles Terrain, elevation change
Website www.great-wall-marathon.com
What it takes Don't be scared; just make sure to come prepared.

Competitors say
❛I've run over 80 marathons across the world, but climbing all those steps was the hardest thing I have ever done.❜

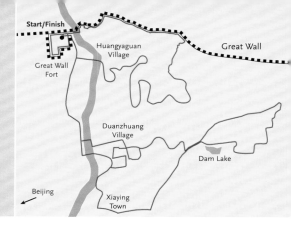

Great Wall Marathon

A total of 5164 steps – some as high as your thigh – with nothing but an age-old handrail stopping you from tumbling down a horrendously steep gradient, as well as heat and physical fatigue, make the Great Wall Marathon unique on the sporting calendar.

below As hard as it is spectacular, the Great Wall Marathon attracts competitors from around the Globe

At one time the Great Wall protected Imperial China from the Mongol hordes who threatened to usurp the ancient dynasty. Some 2000 years later, the wall still stands in its original state (for the most part), a testament to ancient human endeavour. These days, though, rather than soldiers it is patrolled by tourists who swarm to the spectacular fortification from around the world. Anyone who has climbed the wall would immediately know why the Great Wall Marathon earns its place in this book.

Snaking high over mountains before plunging deep into valleys, the wall meanders through the Chinese countryside,

uninterrupted by the folds and falls Mother Nature has thrown in its path. At times it is sedate, a gentle stroll through the hills. Then it rears up, soaring high into the sky before plunging down the side of a mountain. Handrails offer some support, but people do fall – and die – on this wall. And they aren't the ones who are running it.

It is against this backdrop that the Great Wall Marathon takes place. A 42km (26-mile) run that takes its toll on the bodies (and particularly the knees) of those who tackle it. Admittedly, not all the marathon is run on the wall itself. There is a section – uphill, of course – that takes place on asphalt roads, which almost (but not quite) offers a welcome respite for weary legs.

But the race can be defined by the first and third 10km (6 miles) of the marathon. A two-loop course that threads through the Tianjin countryside, these early miles lead up to and along the wall itself. Athletes who take part in the race are faced with a series of steps that ascend and descend along the path of the Great Wall itself. Some of these steps are pretty easy and are little more than ankle high. But others reach as high as your thigh, and that is where it gets difficult.

Climbing 5164 steps is tough enough. Climbing and descending steps that are various heights, occasionally unstable and have little separating you from a nasty fall aside from a loose-fitting handrail requires the utmost concentration. Add to that the physical fatigue that accompanies the marathon, and the pressure this kind of ascending and descending puts on your knees, thighs and ankles is often overwhelming for athletes. That is why the organisers advise participants to wear hiking boots as opposed to running shoes – yet another variable that can offset an athlete's preparation. A lot of athletes in the race choose to walk the steps on the wall. However, those at the business end of the field run them as fast as possible.

And as well as being physically challenging, the heat during the race adds a further variable to factor in. Although it doesn't get excessively hot out on the wall, the sun can be relentless. What's more, in the sections that are not on the wall itself the shade is scant. As such, all competitors have to be prepared to tackle a hot-weather race.

All of this leads to a mentally and physically challenging event. As a result, medical teams monitor participants along the way to ensure they are fit to compete, with some pulled out each year due to their inability to deal with the conditions.

Perhaps all of these variables explain why, on average, participants are told to add an extra 50 per cent to their usual marathon time when taking on the Great Wall Marathon – and the fastest seldom finish in less than six hours.

All things considered, the Great Wall Marathon is a true test of physical and mental endurance. It requires the utmost concentration for half the race and the physical ability to negotiate an uneven and genuinely deadly terrain. This, along with the stress of a marathon-distance race, means that those who cross the finish line feel they have achieved something special and, without doubt, unique.

above The body faces a relentless barrage of steps - both ascending and descending

Henrik Brandt

I have always run a lot. I used to run several times a week. In our local park we have an amphitheatre, so I run up and down and around it to train my legs for the steps.

But this year I had to run in China without any run training at all because of injury. A few months before the race, my wife asked me what my Plan B was because of my injuries and I said, 'There is no Plan B, I have to go to China and I have to do it'.

So I went to China. Of course my injuries hurt all the time, but it was OK. I am always motivated to go to the Great Wall Marathon and finish every year. I don't have to do anything special. I feel it is my race and I have to go there and complete it.

Of course, the steps are tough, but I don't worry about them. When I am on the Great Wall, I do not run the steps. At the

beginning of the race, there are a lot of people, so it is not possible to run and you walk most of the time. Then when you get back to the wall the second time, usually I am exhausted. So I don't worry about the steps. But, of course, the very fast runners do run up and down the steps, and I think that they do have to take care of themselves.

But also you have to go up the mountains and it is very hot – the heat can kill you out there.

Overall, I think it's just amazing. The Great Wall Marathon is the greatest thing for me.

Henrik Brandt is the only person to have competed at – and completed – all 12 of the Great Wall Marathons.

Type Bike
Date March
Distance 400km (248 miles)
Main obstacles Distance, altitude, weather, terrain
Website www.yak-attack.co.uk
They call it A ride that will leave you battered and bruised but with unforgettable memories.

Competitors say
❝It is hugely exciting, and my personal attitude is that you never get so close to living when you're that close to danger.❞

Yak Attack

The highest mountain pass in the world, 12,000m (390,000ft) of vertical climbing, frostbite, snow blindness, routes that are not completely navigable on two wheels – the Yak Attack has every ingredient needed to test the physical prowess of the toughest endurance athletes on the planet, and also make them question their sanity.

below It is a unique introduction to Nepalese culture

From foothills that dwarf any European mountain to mighty peaks that climb higher than the average airplane, the Himalayas cast long shadows across the heart of Asia. And it is through the shadows, the exposed slopes and the meandering tracks that competitors of the Yak Attack must find their way on what is reputed to be one of the toughest mountain bike races on earth.

Taking place over 10 stages and boasting up to 12,000m (39,000 feet) of climbing, the Yak Attack brings together a field of both local and international competitors. But because of the terrain, altitude and weather, the race – and the podium – is more often than not dominated by the Nepalese locals.

Why? Because the physiology of those living at high altitudes is completely different to those of us who live at sea level. So as well as having a natural aerobic advantage, local athletes are also familiar with the challenging terrain and extremes of weather conditions, and understand how to master them all. And that is, ultimately, the true test of the Yak Attack.

There are numerous variables that challenge competitors in the race, with the terrain one of the toughest. Rock, sand, streams, snow and ice present unique challenges that somehow have to be navigated. And unlike most mountain bike races, great swathes of the Yak Attack are simply not rideable (in extreme cases, more than two-thirds of a single stage). This means that as well as carrying the gear needed to complete up to 70km (43 miles)

below Many of the tracks are simply impassable on two wheels

opposite One of the most fearsome race courses in the world

of cycling off-road, competitors are also frequently required to carry their bikes.

This can be challenging enough on flat terrain. But more often than not, the reason the bikes have to be carried is because the paths are too dangerous, too steep or simply impracticable to ride over. Needless to say, walking with a heavy mountain bike and a backpack does not make things much easier.

Of course, the majority of the race can be tackled on two wheels. But that doesn't necessarily mean it is easy. Some 12,000m (39,000 feet) of climbing lends itself to some brutal ascents and some hair-raising descents. Trails are frequently covered with ice or snow, and the drop off the side of them can be steep enough to leave you in pieces (quite literally) at the bottom. Most competitors take multiple tumbles per stage, merely adding injury to the list of variables that have to be factored in when entering the event.

The physicality of the event offers another substantial challenge. Peaking at 5416m (17,769 feet), the race exposes

competitors to conditions where oxygen levels are a mere 50 per cent of that at sea level. As well as immediately making the heart work faster to supply the body with its oxygen needs, these levels are high enough to cause acute mountain sickness (AMS), and people suffering from AMS may feel nauseous, start to get headaches and, in the most extreme cases, die. Add to that the need to ride a bike as hard as possible on stages that generally involve more than 1000m (3280 feet) of vertical ascents (and numerous technical descents) every day, and the physical challenges become clear. This explains why locals do so well in the race. It can take several weeks for a non-acclimatised individual to get used to the oxygen levels at these altitudes. As such, any non-local athlete is already at a disadvantage going into the race.

Of course, the weather in the mountains is also a considerable factor. In the high Himalayas the weather can turn quickly and unexpectedly, and so competitors have to be prepared to race in both temperate conditions and in extreme cold. Temperatures on areas like the Throng La Pass – at 5416m/17,769 feet, the highest navigable pass on the course – can fall as low as −15°C (5°F) before wind chill. All of a sudden, frostbite becomes a very real factor in the minds of participants, and at these temperatures the ability

to control a bike on a technical descent becomes even more challenging.

But these factors are the reason that people choose to tackle the Yak Attack. It is not a leisurely Saturday stroll through the countryside. Instead it is a real, dangerous challenge. The fastest riders can complete the stages in a cumulative time of around 26 hours; the slowest can expect almost to double that. Along the way, all will witness the best and the worst of the greatest mountain range on earth. And all leave the Yak Attack boasting unforgettable memories – and more often than not a few story-worthy scars.

right Exposure to Nepalese culture is another bonus for competitors

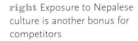

Matt Hart

I didn't know too much about the Yak Attack when I went out there. I knew there would be a lot of altitude, but on reflection if I was to prepare for it again I would have done a lot more hiking and non-bike activities. I had a lot of training volume and I do a lot of bike riding, so I never worried about the cycling. Where I came unstuck was the running/non-cycling preparation.

The other thing that you couldn't prepare for was the altitude. When you do the Yak Attack, the highest point is 5500m (18,000 feet) – the highest mountain pass in the world and about the same as Everest base camp. The stage that took you over that shoulder was a 1000m (3280-foot) climb from 4500m (14,750 feet), all of which was hiking with your kit and bike on your shoulder in the snow. I would literally take five or six steps, stop – and imagine breathing at the hardest you've ever breathed to get oxygen into your system – then 30 seconds later feel great, walk another five steps and be exhausted again. We had to do about 1000m (3280 feet) climbing like that through blizzards and in some pretty treacherous conditions. The altitude you couldn't prepare for, and you had to take it as it came.

The fear of altitude sickness was another factor. You're constantly aware of it at the back of your mind, and if you start getting a headache you need to go back down to a lower altitude, as it can be fatal in a short space of time. So there's fear there.

Also, there were a couple of points on stages where you could easily slide off into oblivion and never be seen again. That is hugely exciting, and my personal attitude is that we're meant to be put into those situations, and you never get so close to living when you're that close to danger. If you do get through these things – which I obviously did – it just leaves its mark.

It really is the adventure of a lifetime. If you're a competitive person and you race, it is brilliant because each stage is a race – you have seven or eight chances of winning it. And that's combined with that the fact that you're in Nepal, which is an eye-opening country. When you land in Kathmandu and meet the people, you get a real deep appreciation of being alive and being surrounded by amazing mountains and really humbling feelings. I got to this 5500m (18,000-foot) shoulder – the highest pass in the world – which is 1000m (3280ft) higher than Mont Blanc and either side of me there are 8000m (26,000-foot) peaks. So you still feel like you're on a valley floor looking up at the Alps, and things like that are so humbling.

Matt Hart is a former professional mountain biker, who conceived Torq Fitness. For more information, visit www.torqfitness.co.uk

ATHLETE PERSPECTIVE

AUST

RALASIA

Type Bike
Date October
Distance 1200km (745 miles)
Main obstacles Terrain, heat
Website www.crocodile-trophy.com
They call it The hardest, longest and most adventurous MTB race in the world.

Competitors say
If you're a cyclist and you want to do one of the most fantastic races in the world, then you have to do the Crocodile Trophy.

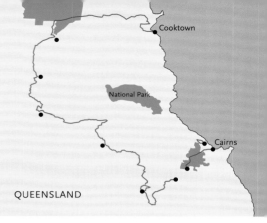

Cooktown

National Park

Cairns

QUEENSLAND

Crocodile Trophy

With 1200km (745 miles) of sand roads, creeks and bush trails beneath a relentless sun, the Crocodile Trophy challenges even the strongest mountain bikers on one of the toughest courses in endurance cycling.

below River crossings add to the challenge

For decades, the Tour de France has inspired cyclists around the world to get out there and ride. But in 1993 Gerhard Schönbacher was inspired to do more than simply get back on the saddle (he rode as a pro from 1982 to 1985). The Austrian decided that he wanted to establish a mountain bike equivalent of the legendary race. At first, he looked at setting up the course in Vietnam. However, when that proved to be unfeasible, he looked back towards home – specifically, the Northern Territory in Australia. Exploration began in earnest soon after, and in a short space of time Schönbacher had determined a start and end point for the first Crocodile Trophy.

But planning the route itself wasn't easy. The Northern Territory can be a fairly remote place. Despite plenty of roads that cut through the bush, uncovering tracks which both challenged the cyclists and also had some sort of habitable area at the end of a stage proved difficult. At times the organisers travelled more than 180km (112 miles) without coming across a single person. However, they persisted and soon the trails for the inaugural Crocodile Trophy were mapped.

The route of the race changes year on year. But the challenges that face the competitors remain the same. Not least, the sheer physical demands of the race itself. On average 1200km (745 miles) long and with more than 13,000m (42,650 feet) of climbing over the course of the ten-day race, this gruelling challenge requires fantastic physical conditioning simply to reach the conclusion of a stage. Any competitor who fails to finish a stage is automatically disqualified from the competition.

Those numbers, though, are simply the top-line statistics. It is once you start to delve into the actual conditions during the course of the race that you begin to realise what is asked of the athletes.

First, there is the terrain. A lot of the race takes place on dirt roads and outback tracks. A lot, but not all. Competitors are also expected to cycle

across creeks – some of which are known to contain the eponymous crocodiles – and stretches of sand that reach up to 50km (31 miles) in length. Not only does that demand an intense physical effort, but there is a lot of practical skill involved in negotiating sand-based roads on a heavy bike while carrying the supplies you need for the stage.

Because while there is support along the way, competitors are expected to carry much of the food, water and equipment that they need to complete the stage themselves (as in any cycle race). This is particularly true in the case of equipment; no outside assistance can be provided to competitors once they are under way. As such, they all have to have the mechanical equipment and know-how needed to fix an ailing bike. This means that a thorough understanding of bike mechanics is an absolute must, as the conditions on the trail mean that it is more than likely that something will go wrong at some stage.

At its heart, the Crocodile Trophy is a race. A serious race. And much like the Tour de France competitors work in packs and attack when they see the right opportunity. The key to finishing each stage – and thus the race – is to understand the nature of pack riding (particularly over tough, variable terrain), and to position yourself in the right pack from the start. This is not always easy and riders can quickly become unpopular if they don't pull their weight or adhere to the unwritten rules of pack cycling.

Master all of the above, and there is a good chance that you can master the Crocodile Challenge. The fastest athletes

complete the course at something close to a 30km/h (18mph) average over the ten stages. Like the race itself, finishing times vary, depending on the difficulty and length of the actual event. But to cycle a mountain bike across variable – often exceptionally challenging – terrain for upwards of 1200km (745 miles) at close to 30km/h (18mph) is an exceptional feat, and provides a sense of the pedigree of the cyclists in this event.

All in, the Crocodile Trophy has achieved what it set out to become: the Tour de France of the mountain bike world. It attracts some of the world's fastest riders (as well as a number of 'mere mortals'), all willing to tackle some of the toughest terrain in a remote unforgiving landscape. It truly is a beast of a race.

left Good technical riding ability is a must

Mike Mulkens

Preparation for the race starts in January (the race is in October) with a goal to peak for the race itself. Of course, some of the riders are professional and race all year round. But while you can prepare physically, you need to also make sure that you are mentally strong. If not, don't bother with the Crocodile Trophy. You suffer on every stage, and there will be moments during the race when you are mentally exhausted and just really happy to reach the finish line.

After three or four days of riding, everybody is tired. But while every stage is tough, the most challenging are the long stages. This year we had one that was 190km (118 miles) long. Everybody was exhausted when they came across the finish line. Because during the race it's not just the distance; it's a combination of feeling tired and the heat. The thing that you can't prepare for is the heat, unless you move to Australia. You can't prepare for it in Europe. That's one of the most difficult parts. The rest you can train for: the hills or the sand, but not for the heat. If your body cannot deal with the heat, then you shouldn't enter.

Some races are described as the toughest or the hardest. But if you look at the Crocodile Trophy you have it all. You have sand parts, river crossings, uphill, downhill ... and phenomenal landscapes. You

see things that are amazing. It's a big adventure. Sometimes you are on a stage and you don't have enough food or water to reach the next depot and then you just try to survive. And sometimes competitors will help you.

The atmosphere in the race is amazing. Of course, everyone who participates wants to get a good overall classification. But it's also about enjoying the adventure. You can go for days without the internet or without phones. There's nothing. If you need to go to the toilet, you're given a shovel and you go to the bush. It's away from society. It's amazing, it's different, it's special.

When I finished and they asked me whether I'd come back next year I said, 'No way, I'm not doing that race again'. But when I got home I forgot about the suffering. Then afterwards I thought about it. The atmosphere was amazing and mentally I started thinking about preparing the next year. There's so much satisfaction at reaching the finish line and I want to go and win a stage, but it is really difficult with the top riders.

If you're a cyclist and you want to do one of the most fantastic races in the world, then you have to do the Crocodile trophy.

Type Multi-discipline
Date February
Distance 243km (150 miles)
Main obstacles Weather, terrain
Website www.coasttocoast.co.nz
They call it The benchmark by which all other multi-sport events are judged.

Competitors say
A very serious undertaking, but with the right frame of mind it is also a fantastic adventure.

TASMAN SEA

Finish

Start

PACIFIC OCEAN

Coast to Coast New Zealand

The path less trodden across some of the most stunning landscape New Zealand has to offer, the Coast To Coast is a true test of human endurance. Competitors tackle cycling, running and kayaking through a beautiful – and brutal – landscape.

below The Waimakariri pushes novice and experienced kayakers alike

Against the twilight backdrop of the Tasman Sea, 100 competitors listen to the gentle thud of the helicopter approach. The sun slowly reaches above the horizon and soon – for some, too soon – that helicopter is upon them. This moment marks the start of the Coast to Coast. A lung-busting, muscle-sapping race straight through the heart of one of the most spectacular countries on earth. En route to the finish line, competitors will cycle along undulating roads and through cosmopolitan cities. They will run over mountains, through forests and across rivers. And they will kayak 67km (41 miles) of a Grade Two river, fighting not only the currents but the howling winds of the Waimakariri Gorge.

Some competitors compete alone, some in teams, and there is the option of a one- or two-day attempt at the course. A few hardy athletes attempt to do the entire race in one day – with the record for completing the Coast to Coast standing at an impressive 10 hours, 34 minutes and 37 seconds set by Keith Murray back in 1994. To post that time, Murray completed 140km (87 miles) of cycling – broken down into stages of 55km (34 miles), 15km (9 miles) and 70 km (43 miles) – as well as 36km (22 miles) of running and 67 km (41 miles) of kayaking in tough conditions.

And it all begins on the beach. A 3km (1.8-mile) run along the sand takes competitors to their bikes, and the beginning of a 55km (34-mile) drag to Aickens Corner. A drafting race, many competitors counteract the headwind on the hilly route by cycling in packs.

But this initial bike is just the aperitif for what promises to be a tough main course. Because once the first bike leg is complete, the footrace begins. And so does the long, tough climb up to the highest point on the course: the 1070m (3500-foot) Goat

Pass. During this ascent competitors not only have to find their way (the course is signposted, though for the most part it is a question of following the tracks of those ahead of you), but must also traverse streams and fast moving rivers. All of this with their day supplies on their back.

The summit of Goat's Pass doesn't offer much respite, though, as the downhill is just as testing on the legs. What's more there are still plenty of rivers and creeks to cross. Every part of the footrace – from the physical to the mental – challenges athletes looking to complete it.

Needless to say, once the footrace is complete it doesn't get any easier. A quick 15km (9-mile) bike takes them to Mount White Bridge and the start of the Kayak. A Grade Two category river, the Waimakariri might not be the technically most challenging stretch of water in the world, but on an already fatigued body it has plenty of fight to punish those not skilful enough to tackle both the currents and the ferocious winds that howl through the Waimakariri Gorge at up to 92km/h (57mph).

The rules and regulations around the kayak leg of the race are tight. Competitors must have certificates to show that they are technically proficient to handle a Grade Two river, and organisers will remove anyone from the water who seems unable to deal with the demands of the fast-moving Waimakariri.

above The winds can be brutal on the bike

above right Athletes are forced to navigate different terrains.

But the river is also an assist to those skilful enough to master her. Competitors kayak with the current, and for those proficient in river kayaking there are fast lines through some of the technical sections. But those lines come with the challenge of the brutal head or side wind, and so the ability to master a boat in tough conditions becomes paramount to finishing this leg.

Finally, the longest cycle leg of the event. Having spent plenty of hours battling the river, athletes hit the 70km (43-mile) stretch back into Christchurch. By this point the numbers are few and far between (so there are no large packs to draft off) and the winds that have plagued competitors in the gorge continue to help – or hinder – on the bike. But home is in sight. Christchurch by and large comes to a halt during the running of the race, and competitors are made to feel like royalty when they do eventually cross the line. And they have earned it.

A solid test of human endurance across a variety of disciplines, the New Zealand Coast to Coast truly pushes athletes to the limits. Taking on some of the toughest terrain and hardest conditions that one of the most beautiful countries on the planet has to offer, finishers can look back on a true endurance challenge.

Kevin Russ

Day One: The blare of the foghorn jolts everyone into go mode, the run from the beach to the bikes a very pleasant diversion from the waiting.

A glorious morning for a bike ride, headwind in our faces at Jacksons. The 55km (34-mile) ride is over pretty soon as I jump off the bike and hobble into the Aickens Corner transition.

The Deception route is just that, a route, no real discernible best path, and there is a roaring stream running through the middle of it all.

Helicopters flying low overhead mean we finally are very close to the top, the rotor wash providing welcome relief on the still, hot day up the final boulder-strewn creek bed. I head past the hut, over the saddle and down into the Minga valley.

I move through the tops, the beech forest, across scree slopes and ultimately out on to the river flats.

I go directly down the middle of the riverbed on some soft sand islands and finally scramble through a deep pool to the finishing chute. I am in pain but get to do the only real running on this leg, the final 50m (165 feet) in the finishing chute. I am knackered and I am elated, I want to lie down for a while.

Day Two: The short bike ride is staged in groups of 10 and finally our group is off; it's great to warm up and the 15km (9 miles) streaks by. The hardest piece of this morning is trying to run down the Mount White bridge access road; thank God there are a few hours of sitting in the kayak coming up.

The gorge is an impressive place to kayak: sheer grey rock faces rise straight out of aqua-green water. I was terrified a lot of the time and in awe of the situation the rest of the time.

The north-westerly, which was building, rips down valleys, carrying swirling dust and hitting boats broadside at up to 50 knots (92km/h, 57mph).

At one stage there are people literally being blown out of their boats around me, people swimming, boats blown like leaves through the air, some people just standing on the bank with nothing, waiting for a jetboat to pick them up, knowing their day is over.

The north-westerly which was such a demon on the river, was suddenly my new best friend; just have to chase down the 70km (44 miles) to the finish. Long straight flat roads and suddenly you enter Christchurch City. Police step out and stop traffic at the major intersections, you feel like royalty.

A sign says 'Only 150 trees to go until a nice cold Speights' and I know I am almost there.

There's lots of noise and suddenly the sand finishing chute I had been dreaming about was in front of me. Finally I can stop. I stand in a daze, not believing it's all over.

Lying in bed later that night in a house on the hill above Sumner, I can't sleep, my body is just radiating heat, I can hear others finishing late into the night. Eventually I fall into a deep sleep with a smile on my face.

NORTH
AMERICA

CANADA

International falls

NORTHERN
MINNESOTA, USA

Pelican Lake

Vermillion Lake

Type Foot, ski or cycle
Date January
Distance 217km (135 miles)
Main obstacles Cold, weather, terrain
Website www.arrowheadultra.com
They call it The historically coldest gosh darn race anyplace ... even the Arctic.

Competitors say
It's mind over matter. If you don't mind, it don't matter.

Arrowhead 135

Brutally cold and fantastically raw, the Arrowhead 135 is as much about survival as it is about completing the grueling 135-mile (217km) course.

Northern Minnesota is a land of extremes. During the summer months, wolves and moose roam freely through the forests and lakes, with eagles and ospreys patrolling the skies. But with the onset of winter, the countryside in the northern state becomes barren and inhospitable. The snow and ice set in early, and the temperature plummets to somewhere between −34°C (−30°F) and −40°C (−40°F), at times touching −51°C (−60°F).

It is against this bitterly cold, unwelcoming environment that the Arrowhead 135 is run. This is a long, challenging and unforgiving race, and only 20 per cent of the 120 starters will typically finish it. And that is regardless of the discipline in which they are racing. Unlike many of the challenges in this book, competitors can choose to tackle the race on foot, by bike or on skis. Each discipline carries with it different qualifying standards (as you might expect, most involve

right Athletes have to be able to survive in the harshest conditions

long-distance races run under similar conditions), ensuring that the field that turns up in January is comprised of some of the world's fittest, fastest and toughest ultra-distance athletes.

That makes the high dropout rate all the more remarkable. But when you start to look into what is demanded of the athletes, you start to see why so many fail to finish.

The cold is unremitting and intense. Regardless of whether the athlete is skiing, cycling or running, maintaining forward momentum in such extremes of temperature is physically and mentally exhausting.

What's more, the race is entirely self-supported. So while shelters with sanitation equipment and fire pits are dotted every 19km (12 miles) along the Arrowhead Trail, to complete the event you have to start with everything that you intend to finish with. And, as you might expect, the list of mandatory equipment is extensive. All athletes are required to carry everything from sleeping materials to cooking equipment, lights, whistles (because the mouth is often too numb to shout) and food. What's more, competitors also have to cross the finishing line with more than 6.8kg (15lb) of emergency gear and 3000 calories of emergency food. That is a solid amount of weight for fatigued and weary limbs to be carrying through the cold.

But at least the track that the race is run on is both clear and sound. Stretching from International Falls in Minnesota to the edge of Lake Vermilion, the Arrowhead Trail is primarily used for snowmobiling in the winter. And at the start of the race the track is relatively welcoming. Flat and rolling, the northern section of the trail winds through forests and over frozen lakes. Then the real fun begins. As the trail heads south, the hills become more frequent and exposed rock surfaces start to become a regular occurrence. The gradient and conditions on parts of this section of the trail begin to take their toll on the athletes, and it is not uncommon for cyclists to be forced to push, and runners be forced to walk where the going gets really tough.

In total, competitors will end up climbing some 2300m (7500 feet) over the 217km (135 miles). Once they have tackled the second section of the race, things get easier. The final 32km (20 miles) are flat to the finish, and those who have made it to this section can rest assured that the hard part is behind them.

But they have to keep on pushing. The cut-off times for the Arrowhead 135 are aggressive. The race starts at 7 a.m., and there are three checkpoints that racers must hit within certain time limits. Checkpoint One is at 56km (35 miles) and must be reached 14 hours after start. Checkpoint Two is at 112km (70 miles), to be reached after 31 hours; and Checkpoint Three, 52 hours after start. The official finish cut-off time is 60 hours after the start.

Of course, as with so many of these events, the winners of the race record exceptional times given the tough

above Managing energy expediture is key to negotiating the terrain and conditions

conditions on the course. The course record on the bike is 15 hours, 50 minutes; on the run, 37 hours, 59 minutes; and on skis, 36 hours, 5 minutes. But these times are for the best of the best. In 2011 nobody on skis managed to finish the race despite a record high number of starters. It is a brutal course.

The Arrowhead 135 pushes athletes to the limits of physical survival. Bitterly cold, a tough course and pretty much entirely self-supported, there's a good reason why the majority of starters fail to finish the race. But for those who do, there is the satisfaction of knowing they have completed an event that has defeated some of the toughest endurance athletes in the world. Enter, those who dare!

John Storkamp and Jeremy Kershaw

ATHLETE PERSPECTIVE

John Storkamp: Obviously, being physically prepared for Arrowhead is critical. In the foot division, having previous ultra-marathon experience is certainly helpful – equally or perhaps more importantly is understanding cold weather and winter.

Jeremy Kershaw: I think the physical preparation is the easiest, actually. Lots of hill workouts. I have a backpack that is loaded with a 27kg (60lb) tube of sand. Mentally, I think that years of winter travel as a dogsledding guide finally paid off. I had the experience to know how I cope with being cold and wet and tired. I rely heavily on that accumulated knowledge to get me to the next checkpoint and to the finish line. I just 'know' that I'll be OK out there.

JS: The mental aspect of doing an event like this cannot be underestimated. Time and space during an event such as Arrowhead can get warped in ways you cannot imagine unless you have experienced it. The sun does not come up until about 7.30 a.m. and it starts getting dark sometime after 4 p.m., so you spend a considerable amount of time travelling in the dark, by yourself. Obviously this is not for everyone and you need to have your head on right.

JK: Time to train in what I would consider 'adequate' chunks is difficult to do as a father of two young kids, husband and full-time RN. There just isn't enough daylight (which is why training in the dark is helpful sometimes ... and good practice).

JS: The race – it's a matter of learning how to be comfortable with being uncomfortable. Eric Johnson – a several time finisher of Arrowhead 135 – has a great quote: 'It's mind over matter. If you don't mind, it don't matter.' And really that's what it is, it's a state of mind – you have to get yourself there and stay there. It's an uncompromising attitude in which you say to yourself, 'There is only one outcome here – it's me finishing this race.'

JK: One of the hardest sections of the race is the very beginning. You are passed by cyclists, skiers and other runners going out too fast. You think, 'I am going to be dead last!' With experience, though, an easy half of these people will not make the finish. It's a race of attrition.

JS: No matter how tough or how experienced you are, you will always have a few issues, hopefully none that surprise you – that is the key. Things that seem like a quick fix at room temperature in 'real life' become nearly impossible at –40°C (–40°F) with no sleep after a hard 160km (100 miles). You have to be willing to accept your current state of affairs, then be flexible enough to adjust – those who are unwilling to be flexible, bend and adjust in a race like this, usually break when difficulties arise.

Finishing a race like Arrowhead is a unique experience. There is very little external fanfare – it's a personal thing ... an inside thing. On one hand you are happy to be done; on the other, you have just experienced some really intense thoughts, feelings and emotions for a couple of days and you have experienced self-reliance and resiliency in its purest form – letting that go and walking inside can be very tough. The experience leaves a mark on you – it's hypnotic and magnetic, it's hard not to go back ...

JK: Completing the walk/run last year was one of the biggest endurance accomplishments of my life. I felt real satisfaction knowing that I was able to keep going – even 'race' – under such tough conditions. It's funny, but as I write this and reflect back on the event, I am really overcome with a sense of pride.

John Storkamp has finished the Arrowhead 135 four times and was the first to do it on foot. Jeremy Kershaw has completed the Arrowhead 135 in all disciplines.

Type Foot
Date June
Distance 160km (100 miles)
Main obstacles Altitude, elevation change
Website www.leadvilleraceseries.com
They call it The race where legends are created
   – and limits are tested.

Competitors say
I think the biggest physical challenge of the race is running at such high altitude.

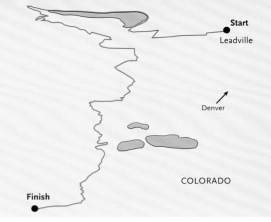

COLORADO

Start
Leadville

Denver

Finish

Leadville 100

High altitude, extremes of temperature and trails that leave the limbs battered and weary, the Leadville 100, or Race Across The Sky, is a journey into the heart of one of the United States' most spectacular – and unforgiving – environments.

below Athletes come prepared for a long day

The prospect of gold attracted the first settlers to Leadville in the 1850s. The harsh winter conditions quickly sent them away. But they returned, and very soon the town of Leadville was born. It was a relatively lawless place, but with the gold in them thar hills it quickly boomed. Over the years, though, the gold dried up, boom turned to bust and by the mid-1980s Leadville boasted the highest level of unemployment in the United States. That gave Kenneth Chlouber and Merilee Maupin an idea. To boost the profile of the town and attract more visitors, they conceived of the 'Race Across The Sky' – a 160km (100-mile) ultra-marathon to test the strength and mettle of the best athletes in the country.

Despite concerns that people might die attempting the route, the race was a resounding success. The early years of the competition laid the foundations for a now legendary event, and one that attracts participants and spectators from around the globe. Attracted by one of the toughest, most demanding races on the planet, athletes come to pit their strength against a course that often sees less than 50 per cent of the starters cross the line before the cut-off time.

The Leadville 100 is not known as the Race Across The Sky for no reason. At its lowest point, athletes are still 2800m (9200 feet) above sea level. Meanwhile, the high point on the course – Hope Pass – sees athletes top out at 3840m (12,600 feet). This places a massive strain on the heart and lungs of any athlete competing in the race, particularly those not acclimatised to altitude. Prolonged periods of exercise at this kind of height can easily lead to nausea, respiratory problems, headaches and impaired performance. As such, this is a key consideration for competitors looking to tackle – and complete – the Leadville 100, with organisers keen to stress the importance of acclimatising to the conditions before race day.

What's more, to make the challenge just that little bit harder, the journey from the lowest to the highest point on the course happens over just 8km (5 miles). That is a cumulative climb of 1040m (3400 feet) in a very short space of time. And competitors face the same descent along the way to the finish line. Because, unlike many ultra-distance races, the Leadville 100 is a straight out-and-back course, with the turning point following a rapid descent of the 3840m (12,600-foot) Hope Pass. As such, when competitors reach this point, not only do they have to run back up the mountain, they must then tackle the demanding descent. This places an enormous amount of strain on already fatigued limbs, with risks heightened by the changing conditions on the route.

The race begins at 4 a.m., but the vast majority of competitors will spend a significant period of time tackling the course at night. The change in temperature in the mountains around Leadville can be severe, with daytime highs of up to 26°C (80°F) and night-time temperatures in the region of −3°C (25°F). What's more, the weather on the course is notoriously variable, and it is not uncommon for athletes to be running in bright sunshine one hour and heavy downpours the next. This means ensuring not only that every competitor has the necessary equipment for cold, wet and night-time running but also that they manage their bodies accordingly. Hypothermia is a very real threat to competitors in the race, particularly those towards the back of the field, and understanding their body's reaction to the variable conditions is key to completing the course, not to mention staying healthy.

The same is true for nutrition and hydration. The humidity in the mountains can be as low as 5 per cent, meaning that athletes are even more susceptible to dehydration than normal. As with all ultra-distance races, managing nutrition and hydration is key to completion, and in the case of the Leadville 100 being allowed even to continue. All competitors are weighed at certain points during the race, and anyone who is found to have dropped more than 7 per cent of their bodyweight is pulled from the event (between 3 and 5 per cent, and medical staff have the right to feed and water competitors until they are back to healthy levels). The challenge may be great but the mountains can be dangerous, and organisers do all that they can to ensure everyone leaves the race healthy and happy.

One man who left the race exceptionally happy was Matt Carpenter, who in 2005 set the course record at an astounding 15 hours, 42 minutes and 59 seconds. The feat was all the more remarkable given that he managed to cross the finish line while

above and right
Altitude, variable conditions, brutal ascents, the Leadville 100 has it all

Ryan Sandes

I live in Cape Town (South Africa) at sea level, so I got to Leadville about five weeks beforehand to acclimatise to the very high altitude of the race. I think the biggest physical challenge of the race is running at such high altitude. The Leadville was also my first 100-miler (160km), so I did a number of really long training runs of five to eight hours. Mentally it's about being out there and enjoying what you're doing.

The biggest challenge in preparation was getting used to the altitude and not overtraining. It took me a lot longer to recover from training at altitude.

I broke the race down into lots of bite-size chunks and would focus on just getting to the next aid station. Once I got to the aid station, I focused on getting to the next aid station, and so on. I enjoyed the surroundings and the race atmosphere, which took my mind off racing. I really wanted to win this race, so I was super-motivated going into the lead for the final 80km (50 miles).

I had a number of highs and lows during the race – a lot of it was mental, and you just have to focus on the positives of running the race. My sugar levels dropped a few times, but I made sure I ate and drank a lot during the race. My quads got very sore in the final 30km (20 miles), but that again was mind over matter.

Wow! It was a dream come true to run the Leadville 100, and winning it was an awesome feeling. I was quite emotional as I ran the final 100m (330 feet) with the South African flag in my hands. Crossing the finish line, I was elated, but physically I was so, so tired. I trained really hard for the race, so winning it was very rewarding.

Ryan Sandes has won numerous ultra-distance races around the world – including the 2011 Leadville 100. For more information, visit ryansandes.com

the sun was still shining – the first time anybody had ever been able to do so.

The Leadville 100 is a test on every level. From the high altitudes to brutal descents (not to mention ascents), it is a thorough test of body, heart and mind for every competitor who tackles the challenge, and for a significant number the test is too hard. But that is what makes the race one of the greats. And for those who complete the epic course, a place in the history books beckons.

Type Foot
Date August
Distance 160km (100 miles)
Main obstacles Heat, terrain, elevation change
Website www.ws100.com
They call it One of the oldest ultra trail events in the world and certainly one of the most challenging.

Competitors say
"Heat, altitude and brutal ascents and descents – the Western States 100 is a course that routinely gets the better of the horses that race the route, let alone the humans."

CALIFORNIA

Squaw Valley

Lake Tahoe

Auburn

Western States 100

The Tevis Cup is renowned for its brutality. The race has routinely got the better of riders and their horses since 1955, when Wendell Robie first conquered the route. However, in 1974, Gordy Ainsleigh thought he would raise the bar.

below The weather is as taxing as the course

Ainsleigh had completed the Tevis Cup in 1971 and 1972, but in 1973 he was forced to withdraw from the event when his horse pulled up lame. That gave him an idea: rather than rely on a horse to complete the race, why not see if he could run it himself? The course would be the same, the time limit the same, the challenges exponentially harder. On a blisteringly

hot day that unfortunately claimed the life of at least one horse, Ainsleigh completed the 'quasi-suicidal' challenge in 23 hours, 42 minutes. He had proven to himself and the race organisers that it could be done.

In the years that followed, two men attempted to complete the race; only one of them did. Then in 1977 the official Western States Endurance Run took place. Fourteen men started alongside the horses in the Tevis Cup, and three of them finished. Only the winner, Andy Gonzales, finished within the 24-hour cut-off limit. Because of this, the decision was made to extend the cut-off time to 30 hours (or 11 a.m. the next morning). In the following year the run separated from the ride (it is now run a month earlier), and since then the status quo has pretty much remained the same. As have the challenges that face the athletes along the route.

The weather, altitude and trails of the Western States 100 are enough to get the better of all but the toughest ultra-distance runners. With a starting point in the Squaw Valley, which sits at 1900m (6200 feet), the run immediately climbs more than 780m (2550 feet) in just 7km (4.5 miles). This is only the beginning. Throughout the duration of the race competitors can expect to ascend more than 5500m (18,090 feet) and descend 7000m (22,970 feet) over the 160km (100-mile) course. Along the route they will pass through canyons, over the top of mountains and tackle trails with sheer vertical drops off one side or another.

The distance, coupled with the severity of the ascents and descents and the high altitude the race is run at, is enough to test most athletes' inner reserves. But perhaps the most challenging aspect of the race is the climate. The

left The course weaves its way through incredible scenery

above Every aspect of the course challenges competitors

weather – and the temperatures – in the mountains can vary dramatically. With the race starting out at 5 a.m., it is not uncommon for competitors to be waiting for the starting gun in sub-zero temperatures. What's more, pretty much every athlete competing in the race will have to tackle the latter parts of the course at night-time.

But the cold is often an unpleasant aside to the real concern: the heat. The route the course takes is susceptible to wild fires because it is so hot and dry. The earth soaks up the heat from the sun and throws it back at the athletes, and in the canyons temperatures can easily exceed 43°C (110°F). As such, every athlete has to be capable of dealing with massive extremes of temperature. This affects all aspects of their race, from equipment to nutrition and hydration, and all are essential for its successful completion.

Given the challenges the athletes face, as well as the popularity of the event, organisers have been forced to put in a series of qualification requirements for anyone considering entry. To do so, prospective competitors must have completed a recognised qualification event, and also have met the minimum time criteria of 80km (50 miles) in under 11 hours, 100km (62 miles) in under 14 hours or a 160km (100-mile) trail race within the official cut-off time. If, and only if, an entrant has met these criteria are they eligible for the lottery system, where names are drawn out of the hat. Because of local regulations, the number of competitors is limited to 369 every year – hence the stringent controls.

But this also means that the performances of those involved tend to be of a certain standard. The number of finishers within the 30-hour cut-off time varies from year to year, but tends to hover around the 65–70 per cent mark. The records for the run are, however, extraordinary. Geoff Roes holds the men's record time of 15 hours, 7 minutes and 4 seconds, set in 2010. Meanwhile, Ann Transon's 1994 record of 17 hours, 37 minutes and 51 seconds still stands for the women.

Those who finish within 24 hours are awarded a silver buckle; and within 30, a bronze buckle. But for all of those who complete the event there is the knowledge that they have conquered a course that has bested some of the sturdiest horses in the world in some of the toughest conditions North America has to offer.

Karl Hoagland and Ellie Greenwood

Karl Hoagland: You learn if you get a place the prior December. From that point forwards, your mind never lets you forget you have a date with destiny in six months. That is really exhilarating but also scary, and it is always in your psyche. Whenever you have a free or open brain moment, the race always floods into that space, and you become obsessed with it.

Ellie Greenwood: I mostly trained on my own, which I think is good mental preparation, as it is tougher to go out for long runs on your own rather than having the company of friends and training partners. I didn't tend to go for super long runs and would say that my longest runs were probably not much over five hours. However, I would run back to back runs of four-to-five hours on both Saturdays and Sunday, so learned to run on tired legs that way.

KH: During the race it isn't that hard to keep going – the time just flies by, especially as your consciousness separates from your body and you become just a spectator. But if you do get in tough patches you just have to keep moving forwards and try to stay present and positive. The happiest place is the finish line, but the second happiest place is the starting line – knowing that all the preparation and anticipation is over and that all you have to do is run 160km (100 miles) is a massive relief.

EG: Western States was my first 100-miler, so however good or bad the race unfolded I knew it would be an achievement just to say that I made it to the finish line. Of course, I had much higher goals than simply finishing, but I had this other basic goal, which I hoped would be totally achievable, of just making it to the finish in the cut-off time.

KH: The finish line is sheer joy. On reflection it is a bit of a let-down, and you realise all you really have is your memories, and the shared experiences are what remains and what is most real after the fact. That's part of why I always cross the finish line with all of my crew and pacers holding hands – it is a group accomplishment and sharing it with others makes it many times better and more memorable.

EG: I truly did not believe that I had won the race until I was across the finish line. I ran a very strong final 30km (19 miles) or so of the race, but at 10km (6 miles) to go I was still in third place and about nine minutes back from first. By about 5km (3 miles) I had taken the lead, but I didn't dare believe that I was going to win until I actually had. One key thing I learnt is that the race truly is not over until the end. In such long races, it is often tempting to think you know who will win before it happens, but I ran a very strong finish and in some ways defied the odds of winning. In this respect I learnt that staying focused right until the end and never giving up truly are important, not only for winning but also for performing to the best of your ability.

Karl Hoagland has finished the Western States 100 on multiple occasions. Ellie Greenwood won the race in 2011 on her first attempt.

Type Swim | **Date** Year-round
Distance 35km/22 miles
Main obstacles Distance, currents, cold
Website www.swimcatalina.com
They call it The only major channel crossing on the American continent which compares to the English Channel in both distance and difficulty.

Competitors say

❝My philosophy at the time was in part like a physics experiment; my method was to just keep my body in motion.❞

Santa Barbara

Malibu

Rancho Palos Verdes

Finish

Start

Santa Catalina Island

Catalina Channel Swim

Huge Ocean swells, bitterly cold water, predatory sharks and all in the dead of night. The Catalina Channel Swim is not just an immense physical challenge, but a mental one too.

below The water varies in temperature and ferocity

Captain Matthew Webb has a lot to answer for. In 1875 Captain Webb became the first man to swim the English Channel, setting a benchmark for long-distance swimmers around the world. Just over 50 years later, New Yorker Gertrude Ederle not only became the first woman to swim the Channel, but at 14 hours, 39 minutes she became – at the time – the fastest person to have completed the crossing. Overnight Ederle became a hero both at home and abroad. And one man who was particularly interested in her exploits was William Wrigley (of chewing gum fame). Wrigley was inspired by Ederle and, coupled with his interest in Catalina Island, decided to launch a race across the Catalina Channel: from Santa Catalina Island to Point Vincente off LA. In 1927, 102 swimmers took to the water off Avalon, vying for the

$25,000 winner-takes-all prize purse. Only one person finished the race: George Young.

It took Young 15 hours, 44 minutes, 30 seconds to complete the 35km (22-mile) swim – although it is estimated that he swam further than that due to navigation difficulties. Along the way, he faced heavy ocean swells, kelp beds, the ever-present threat of shark attacks, jellyfish stings and strong tidal flows. Today's swimmers face exactly the same challenges, which explains why just over two hundred people have managed to complete the swim since Young first made the crossing.

Like the English Channel, the Catalina Channel Swim is open to anyone and can be tackled at any time of the year. Usually, due to weather and conditions, competitors attempt the swim between late spring and the end of summer, when the water temperature varies from 15 to 21°C (60–70°F). However, the water temperature drops as athletes approach the mainland. Exercising for a prolonged period of time in cold water provides one of the fundamental challenges for any athlete wanting to take on the Catalina.

Like all long-distance swims, the Catalina Channel is a non-wetsuit affair. Athletes are stripped back to basics, swimming in just a swimsuit, goggles and cap. As such, athletes must be prepared to deal with the demands of

excercising in cold water. Even so, the threat of hypothermia is ever present in the swim, and many athletes succumb to the fatigue induced by the relentless exposure.

An exposure that is made all the more uncomfortable due to the water conditions in the channel. From the get-go, things are not easy. To properly complete this long-distance swim you need to start from a point where there is no water behind you, and finish at a point where there is no water ahead of you. To achieve this in the Catalina Channel, swimmers must negotiate sharp rocks and ocean swells. Swells that only increase after leaving the relative shelter provided by Santa Catalina Island.

The Pacific Ocean rolls through this channel, and swells of 1.5–2.5m (5–8 feet) are common. This perpetual rolling motion can take its toll on the swimmer, with many succumbing to seasickness. Of course, every swimmer who tackles the Catalina must be supported by a guide kayak (who is there to provide food, drink and navigation, but nothing more). However, with most attempts at the swim starting at night, navigation is complicated enough without the added factor of rolling seas.

The unusual timing of the event – largely down to the lack of shipping traffic in the Channel as well as favourable wind conditions – places an added stress upon the swimmer, who is unable to see any discernible landmarks for up to six hours during the swim.

But no description of the challenges faced when crossing the channel would be complete without some mention of what lurks beneath. Many swimmers and their support teams revel in dolphin, seal and occasional whale sightings. They rarely talk about the sharks and jellyfish. While the threats of sharks offers – for the most part – psychological barriers, jellyfish stings are common and an uncomfortable accompaniment to the crossing.

Of course, despite the challenges, or perhaps because of them, the accomplishments are immense. Of the two hundred or so individuals to complete the crossing, Penny Dean's 1976 record of 7 hours, 15 minutes and 55 seconds

below Passing traffic pays little heed to ambitious swimmers

opposite A support team can provide nutrition, hydration and navigation

still stands as the fastest. The slowest so far recorded is an impressive 33 hours, 50 minutes, an incredible period of constant submersion in cold water.

But that is the beauty of the Catalina Channel. She brings out the best in people facing up to an extraordinary challenge. She doesn't make it easy for those who take her on, and the challenges merely get tougher the further into the swim an athlete gets. But for those who complete this epic trial, there is safety in the knowledge that they have done what few before them have managed – despite the many who have tried. Yes, the Catalina Channel Crossing is without a doubt one of the toughest swims on the planet.

Rendy Lynne Opdycke

On Saturday, 9 August, 2008, I swam the Catalina Channel, from Catalina to the California mainland, in 8 hours, 28 minutes. This was the third fastest directional time for a woman and the sixth fastest time overall out of 145 people who have swum the channel solo since 1927.

With this swim, I became only the second swimmer to accomplish the Triple Crown in less than a year. I completed all three swims in 34 days, the shortest period ever recorded. On 5 July, I completed the Manhattan Island Marathon, English Channel on 27 July and Catalina on 9 August. My total swimming time for completing the three is also the fastest ever, at 26 hours, 50 minutes.

The Catalina was the toughest to prepare mentally, not because it was the last of the Triple Crown, but because it was emotionally attached to my dad's death – the day he died, I had just landed from escorting my second swimmer for their crossing. This was probably the toughest swim I have ever done – not physically, not mentally, but totally emotionally.

I did not really face any obstacles physically, as I was confident that I was in top form from the MIM and English Channel. In part I did not think about what I was facing until I actually was at the shore, loading up the boat for the Catalina Channel – and it hit me, hard. Although, I was a wee bit tired from the swim around Manhattan Island, then flying across the pond to conquer the English Channel and dealing with the time changes back from England to Catalina prior to the swim. Those external stresses were nothing compared to the emotional bond I had to face with the Catalina Channel and the emotional quest I was about to embark on.

I believe that to be a successful open-water marathon swimmer an athlete should employ their own methodology of actively distracting themselves when the feat starts to become challenging, to remain in good spirits. In the case of marathon swimming, as I am sure is the same as other marathon events, your brain becomes your own worst enemy.

Personally, I enjoyed the bioluminescent algae lightshow that occurred during the wee hours of the morning; swimming with Risso's dolphins was also rather an excitement. Drawing from my history, I've become used to the afternoon chop that picks up from windy conditions. One shock to the system was about 9km (4 nautical miles) offshore: the temperature naturally drops a few degrees and after that the body starts to begin to fatigue – it becomes a mental issue, and I've learned to adapt to it.

I had no idea I had set records as to the fastest time for the three swims, nor the shortest amount of time for the swims being accomplished. Other people keep track of those stats – I swim around islands and across channels because I love the sport and I hope others will join in the wonders of ocean swimming.

Rendy Lynne Opdycke is the Triple Crown Record Holder, having completed the Catalina Channel, English Channel and Manhattan Island Marathon Swims in the shortest combined times and within the shortest time frame.

Type Bike
Date June
Distance 4828km (3000 miles)
Main obstacles Distance, mental, elevation change
Website www.raceacrossamerica.org
They call it The world's toughest bike race.

Competitors say
❛RAAM strips you to your core. It's a lonely experience in many ways but puts a mirror up to you and reflects the person you are.❜

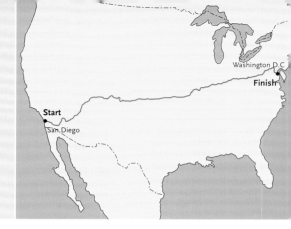

Washington D.C
Finish
Start
San Diego

Race Across America

Massive distances, a ridiculous amount of vertical miles covered, sleep deprivation and an aggressive cut-off time lie in store for those attempting the world's toughest cycle race: the Race Across America.

The Race Across America (RAAM) is one of those pinnacles of athletic achievement that should be in every endurance athlete's bucket list. Traversing North America, the race starts on the West Coast at Oceanside Pier, California, and finishes on the East at Annapolis, Maryland. En route, competitors take in 4828km (3000 miles) of road, master 51,800m (170,000 feet) of vertical climbing and pass through 12 US states.

The challenge of riding a bicycle across the United States was first completed in 1887 by newspaperman George Nellis. Nellis used an iron bike with no gears, and pedals attached to the front wheel. Using the railroad routes to guide him across the continent, the crossing took him just under 80 days. Although this record was improved steadily over the years, it wasn't until 1982 that a group of riders decided they were ready for a head-to-head race across the country, starting on the Santa Monica Pier in Los Angeles and racing

to the Empire State Building in New York. With national television coverage the race caught the public's imagination, and since then it has taken place every year. With the addition of relay teams in 1992, the event became accessible to any reasonably fit cyclist, further increasing its popularity.

What makes RAAM so special is that it is a continual time trial race, unlike professional events such as the Tour de France or Vuelta a España, which are broken down into a number of stages. Once riders start, the clock keeps ticking until they cross the finish line. They have just 12 days to complete the route, and anyone finishing after that time fails to register an official finish. In this respect, RAAM is not only longer than the Tour de France, but competitors have less than half the time to finish. Needless to say, given that RAAM is an amateur race, not everyone who starts out from Oceanside makes the finish.

below Day and night, the cyclists push on whatever the weather

above The route
takes in the best
of America

The distance the riders need to cover is, of course, the major obstacle in the race. But with that distance comes other challenges: most notably the need to balance sleep with the demand to keep moving. The fastest finishers take just over eight days, riding 400–560km (250–350 miles) per day with less than two hours' rest. As a result, the toll of sleep deprivation is a constant danger, with those hoping to simply finish within the cut-off time rarely able to sleep for more than four hours a day.

Keeping the body going for this length of time also requires a significant amount of fuelling, with riders easily drinking 14l (3 gallons) of fluid a day and consuming 300–400 calories per hour (more than 8000 calories per day). To manage these aspects each rider needs a support crew who will provide them with the key nutrition, fluids, navigation, clothing changes, bike repairs and motivation (along with whatever else they need to realise their goal). As such, RAAM becomes a significant logistical operation to manage, and the costs of participating in the event can start at around $20,000.

But the brutal physical challenge – not to mention high costs – do not deter the dedicated from having a go at the race. Of course, as with every race, entry is no guarantee of completion, and only 200 solo (or tandem) racers have officially completed RAAM at the time of writing. Compare that to the 2000 people who have summited Mount Everest,

above The view is stunning, the race brutal

right Relief at the end of a gruelling challenge

opposite Finishing within the cut-off time is something few experience

and you begin to get a feel for the difficulty of the event. The introduction of two-, four- and eight-person relay teams makes the course more manageable. However, the stars of the show are the solo riders who complete the entire journey in one long, arduous go.

Due to course changes, performances are difficult to compare for establishing records. The usual metric used is average speed, rather than total time, with the fastest men's speed by Pete Pensevres in 1986, who rode 5000km (3107 miles) at an unbelievable average of 24.8km/h (15.4mph) in a little over 8 days, 9 hours. The fastest woman was Seana Hogan in 1995, who averaged 21.3km/h (13.23mph) to finish 4686km (2912 miles) in 9 days, 4 hours. In terms of wins, the all-time record holder is the late Jure Robic of Slovenia, who won the race five times before being killed in 2010 in a collision with a car while training for the Crocodile Trophy in Australia.

One obvious question is: How do the race organisers stop people

from cheating? RAAM's answer is to have 53 time stations (many of which are manned at private houses or bike shops) approximately 65–145km (40–90 miles) apart, requiring riders to call in and report their location and time to race headquarters. This allows officials and fans to track the progress of competitors and ensure competitors are riding honest.

What possesses people to tackle an event like RAAM is hard to pin down. Whether to raise money for charity (well over $1m is raised every year) or to prove a point to themselves, something must be driving cyclists who climb from 51m (170 feet) below sea level to 3000m (10,000 feet) above it, cover 4825km (3000 miles) and do it all sleep-deprived and with the pressure of a tough cut-off time limit hanging over them. You want to prove yourself one of the toughest athletes out there? RAAM will definitely give you that opportunity.

Jim **Rees**

I first completed RAAM as part of a four-person team in 2005 and we came in fourth overall. Watching the individual finishers that year, standing on the podium looking completely exhausted, was the inspiration for me to consider an attempt at the solo race. Having qualified for it by being part of a finishing team, I focused on the solo race in 2007.

My training regime was intensive, with the main aim to get used to cycling with sore legs; I averaged 3–6 hours a day, 6 days a week. On Fridays I used to ride 5–6 hours, get home for dinner, head off again at 10 p.m., riding through the night until 4 a.m., sleep for a couple of hours and then go out for another six-hour cycle. Then on Sunday I would go for a ride with the local cycling club. This build-up led to my first successful completion of RAAM in 2007, which was a thrill to finish, though looking back I realised I spent too much time fiddling around off the bike, enjoying the experience and thanking marshals as opposed to just focusing on the riding.

For my next attempts in 2008 and 2009, I made sure the only time I spent off the bike was for sleeping or using the toilet. In 2009, for just over 10 days of riding I had only about 13^{1}/$_{2}$ hours of sleep. My training also changed for these later races. Instead of all the volume from 2007 – where I believe I overtrained – I focused more on quality in an effort to increase speed.

In 2009 I was chasing the British record and was on course until halfway. A few things happened, though, which impacted my final time: I became over-hydrated and my face and hands were swollen from it, which held me back. A storm then flooded the roads, meaning I had to stop for 5 hours. This pushed me behind record pace and then my neck muscles went with 1600km (1000 miles) to go and I couldn't hold my head up without using my hand. So it was an extremely difficult last section, which lost me time as well.

I think to complete the race, it's a matter of having the right mindset and really believing you can do it. I'm just a normal guy, not an Olympic athlete, and have children and a business to run, but I did it through believing in myself and just doing it. I now like to inspire people to believe in what is possible for them.

RAAM strips you to your core. It's a lonely experience in many ways but puts a mirror up to you and reflects the person you are.

Jim Rees has finished the solo Race Across America three times (2007, 2008, 2009) and completed the race as part of a team in 2005.

Type Swim
Date June
Distance 45.8km (28.5 miles)
Main obstacles Currents, cold
Website www.nycswim.org
They call it The longest and premier swimming race of the season.

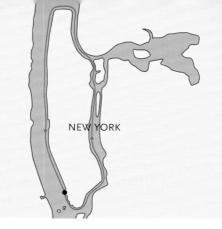

NEW YORK

Manhattan Island Marathon Swim

The stage is iconic, the act brutal. The Manhattan Island Marathon Swim is a true test of human endurance, pitting only the fittest swimmers against the currents, debris and surrounds of the Hudson, Harlem and East Rivers.

The most iconic borough of New York and home to nearly two million people, Manhattan is what most of the world pictures when they think of the Big Apple. An island separated from the other four boroughs that constitute New York City, Manhattan is surrounded by three major rivers: the Hudson, the Harlem and the East River. At times dangerous, at times serene and sometimes downright dirty, these rivers are where one of the toughest swimming events on the planet is played out: the Manhattan Island Marathon Swim (or MIMS).

Launched in 1982 by New York entrepreneur (and excellent swimmer) Drury Gallagher, MIMS was at first resisted by the New York establishment, which deemed the waters around the island too dangerous to swim in. Now, however, this brutal 45.8km (28.5-mile) counterclockwise swim around the island sits proudly as one third of the so-called Triple Crown of distance-swimming events.

The field is small: just 40 athletes and their support crews start the race. To be among that 40 who take to the water at South Cove in Battery Park, you need to have met the qualifying standards for the race: athletes must have either completed one of the other two Triple Crown events (the English Channel crossing or the Catalina Channel crossing) or the Ederle swim within two years of the start date, or have completed an observed open-water swim of more than four hours under similar conditions.

It is these qualifying standards, and the conditions that competitors face in the race, that have helped MIMS to earn legendary status.

The average water temperature on race day is a relatively balmy 21°C (70°F) – although it has been known to hit nearly 26°C (80°F) at times. This is just as well because swimmers are permitted to use only one swimsuit, goggles, earplugs, race cap (a second is optional) and grease.

Throughout the duration of the swim, each competitor is accompanied by a support crew, who can hand over food and drink. But at no point can a support crew aid the swimmers physically other than to pull them out of the water if they are incapable of completing the race. Any non-sanctioned physical contact leads to an automatic disqualification.

But the role of the support crew is much more than simply providing the swimmers with their food and drink.

below New York, New York!

They are, essentially, guides. The natural obstacles posed by the confluence of three rivers are testing enough, but the man-made obstacles can be just as dangerous. While the race itself is a testament to the clean water around Manhattan, there is still plenty of flotsam and jetsam to negotiate, river traffic to avoid, and a sewage treatment plant to pass. The swimmers know the route and the scenery, but it is much more difficult to spot debris and obstacles from water level when severely fatigued than it is from a kayak or boat.

There is, however, little that the support crew can do about the tide. The reason that the race is held anticlockwise is because of the strong tidal movement of the rivers around Manhattan. That does not, however, mean that swimmers are always tide-assisted. Quite the opposite, in fact. Because where the rivers meet and the currents strengthen, even the strongest athletes are forced to push hard to maintain forward momentum.

And they have to maintain that momentum to reach the checkpoints in time. From South Cove athletes have to reach the Triborough Bridge within 3 hours, 30 minutes; Spuyten Duyvil within 5 hours, 45 minutes; 79th Street Boat Basin in 7 hours, 30 minutes; and Pier 26 within 9 hours, 10 minutes. The cut-off times are aggressive, and they are adhered to strictly.

Needless to say, all of this places an incredible strain on the body. The constant exertion of swimming 45.8km (28.5 miles) is hard enough without having to deal with the various waterborne obstacles that athletes come across as

below The landmarks en route are spectacular

they swim. But for those who do compete in the swim, they are part of a race that has it all: Wall Street, the Empire State Building, Brooklyn Bridge and the UN Building are just a few of the notable landmarks that swimmers pass. Along the way, crowds are famous for cheering and clapping the competitors, and the reception they get as they make their way back to South Cove is immense. It is, quite simply, an unforgettable New York experience.

The winner takes home the prestigious Gallagher Cup, with the top two finishers earning the right to return in September in an attempt to break the course record. Not surprisingly, that record is a frighteningly fast 5 hours, 45 minutes and was set by Australian Shelley Taylor Smith in 1995. British super-swimmer Julie Bradshaw added a twist to the event, completing it in 9 hours, 28 minutes swimming only butterfly.

Regardless of how the race is completed, those who do finish the Manhattan Island Marathon Swim know that they have conquered one of the world's toughest endurance events. A brutal distance played out in challenging conditions beneath one of the world's most spectacular skylines, MIMS is a truly iconic race.

Erica Rose

I prepare both mentally and physically by setting a training plan and sticking to it. When training for the Manhattan Island Marathon Swim, I was also working a full-time job, volunteering at least one night per week and travelling quite frequently on weekends. If I missed a workout, there would be no chance for me to make it up, so I had to be diligent about sticking to my plan. I swam at least 6000m (20,000 feet) each morning of the week before going to work. Tuesday and Thursday evenings, I went to the gym after work and did 45 minutes of 'cardio' followed by 45 minutes of a strength circuit focused primarily on core body exercises and plyometric type movement. On Wednesday evenings, I did yoga. Saturday mornings were my 'long swim' days. Those swims ranged anywhere from about 10,000m (33,000 feet) to lake swims of three to four hours.

The single biggest obstacle for me was figuring out how to train while working full time. There is a huge difference between training for ultra-marathon swims as your sole focus, and training for the same distance swim while working a full-time job and dealing with all of the other obligations one encounters in the 'real world'.

I love open-water swimming and I thrive on challenges. Those two factors keep me going when things get tough during a long swim. If I get to a point where I'm struggling, I start thinking about all of the training I've done and I remind myself that when my body feels tired, my mind will get me through. I'm tough and I'm driven and I do not give up easily – those characteristics are incredibly important in an open-water swimmer. In addition, I have a tremendous support network of coaches, family and friends who believe in me and who have helped me to achieve my goals.

The most difficult part of the Manhattan Island Marathon Swim for me was the last leg through the Hudson River. I was mentally prepared for it to be a bit more boring than the rest of the race because I knew I wouldn't be passing quite as much interesting scenery. I also knew my arms would be tired after five or six hours of swimming. What I did not realise, however, was how much wind and chop I would encounter. I was not prepared for the water and air conditions and I really struggled to stay positive. It was at this point that I most heavily relied on my crew.

Winning the Manhattan Island Marathon Swim felt incredible. I had no idea what to expect going into the competition – I wasn't sure whether I had done enough training to make it seven to eight hours in the water, and I had no idea how I would compare to the other athletes in the race. The fact that I felt strong throughout the entire swim and was able to complete one of the notorious open-water marathon swims in the world after several years away from elite-level open-water swimming was incredibly rewarding. Best of all, I had a lot of fun with the MIMS. I enjoyed the experience from start to finish, and I can honestly say that it is one of my favourite open-water swims.

Erica Rose won the Manhattan Island Marathon Swim in 2011 and has represented the USA on the National Open Water Swimming Team for 12 years. Erica is one of the world's premier marathon swimmers. For more information, visit www.ericaroseswimming.com.

Type Horse
Date August
Distance 160km (100 miles)
Main obstacles Terrain, heat
Website www.teviscup.org
They call it The world's most difficult equestrian endurance ride.

Competitors say
❝I was a bit surprised at the miles and miles – and miles – of cliffs we rode alongside ... cliffs with drops of 150–300m (500–1000 feet) drops right beside the 60cm (2-foot) wide path we trotted along.❞

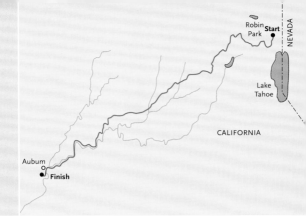

Robin Park · Start
NEVADA
Lake Tahoe
CALIFORNIA
Auburn
Finish

Tevis Cup Ride

From snow-filled passes to sweltering canyons, the Tevis Cup challenges horses and their riders to take on a thrilling – and, at times, treacherous – journey across some of North America's most unforgiving terrain.

They said it couldn't be done. And that is exactly what motivated Wendell Robie, an American businessman and keen horseman, to ride with some friends from Lake Tahoe to Auburn, California one August day back in 1955. The ride was dangerous, it was tough, but it was possible. And after completing that epic feat, Robie decided he would do it again next year. Then again the year after. Soon, the Western States Trail Ride had become a permanent fixture on the endurance-riding calendar, and the Tevis Cup was born.

Renowned throughout the world for being a gruelling test of both human and horse endurance, the Tevis Cup pits riders against a 160km (100-mile) course that includes over 5100m (17,040 feet) of climbing and 6700m (21,970 feet) of descent. All of this must be completed in just 24 hours. For the most part, the route of the race follows the trail Robie originally set out on. There are slight deviations nowadays (largely due to population growth), but the challenges fundamentally remain the same.

To complete the race – let alone compete for the win – riders have to display excellent physical endurance and also supreme horsemanship. In fact, horse management is the most important element of the Tevis Cup. Veterinary tests on the horses are a regular occurrence throughout the race, and at predefined checkpoints athletes must present their horse with a heart rate of less than

left The race requires supreme horsemanship

The route is
often perilous

But to manage a horse along such a gruelling trail is tough. The route of the ride follows a particularly taxing and often technical section of the Western States Trail, which stretches from Salt Lake City, Utah to Sacramento, California.

Beginning south of Truckee, California at the Robie Equestrian Park, with an elevation of 2133m (7000 feet), the trail descends for 14km (9 miles) to the Truckee River. The race then follows a route through Squaw Valley, site of the 1960 Winter Olympics, and ascends from the valley floor at 1890m (6200 feet) to 2667m (8750 feet), a vertical climb of 777m (2550 feet) in 67km (42 miles). From this point riders ascend another 4730m (15,540 feet) and descend almost 7000m (23,000 feet) before reaching the 100-year-old town of Auburn. Large portions of the trail pass along narrow mountain paths – some little more than 1m (3 feet) wide – bordered by a sheer drop to the rocks below. The ride is, at times, incredibly treacherous, and the footing of the horse essential to prevent serious injury to both animal and human.

60 beats per minute and a respiration rate of less than 48 breaths per minute. Failure for a horse to meet these standards means that the animal – and so the rider – is pulled from the race. There are further veterinary checks after the race, and the failure to meet all predefined regulations leads to disqualification.

This might go some way to explaining the low completion rate of the event. From 1955 to 2009, 8920 people started the Tevis Cup. Only 4850 finished. That gives the Tevis Cup a completion rate of just over 50 per cent, with a pretty much even split between male and female riders. But these regulations are essential to the ongoing success of the race. The choice of horse, and the management of its well-being during the event, is essential to the safe and successful completion of the Cup.

But it is not just the technicality of the ride that tests both the rider and the horse. The temperatures en route vary dramatically, and in the canyons can easily top 48°C (120°F). This places immense physical strain on both the rider and the horse, making technical ascents and descents all the more difficult. That is why most riders opt to enlist the help of a support crew. This crew can assist the rider and the horse with food, nutrition and rest at predefined checkpoints (although the rider must present the horse to the veterinarians when required). As with so many of the endurance challenges in this book, the Tevis Cup is something of a team effort.

The winner of the race receives, as you might expect, the Tevis Cup. In addition the Haggin Trophy is awarded to the horse considered to be in the best physical condition of the first 10 finishers. Every rider who completes the race within the 24-hour time limit (and whose mount is judged fit) is awarded the Silver Completion Award Buckle.

While much of the skill involved in the Tevis Cup pertains to horse riding and management, it is also an intensely physical event for the human involved. As well as managing the horse, they have to manage their own fatigue and performance in the heat, and do so over an extended period of time. The sheer challenge of the event is evident in the low number of riders who actually walk away with the Silver Buckle. The mental and physical strain of the Tevis Cup marks this out as a true test of human – and animal – endurance.

Merri Melde

My Tevis adventure is a bit unusual in that, unlike most people who spend months – or years – preparing themselves and their horses for the ride, I had exactly four-and-a-half days of mental and physical preparation. While I'd ridden several thousand AERC miles and completed 200-milers (320km) over my endurance career, I'd never expected I'd get a chance to ride Tevis. I have never had my own endurance horse; I have always ridden for other people. Tevis never crossed my mind. I can't afford to lease a horse, and it's difficult (though not impossible) to find someone to give you a horse to ride. Then there is the huge responsibility you have when you ride someone else's horse. Riding 160km (100 miles) isn't a game on the easiest of courses, and Tevis is particularly challenging for a horse. So Tevis was so far off my radar it was never even a dream.

I had planned to go to Tevis to report on it for Endurance.net. On Monday before Tevis, my friend Nance called me out of the blue with an offer to ride her horse Big Sky Quinn, when her other friend had to back out because of work conflicts. I was quite stunned. I didn't know what to say. I said 'Yes!' and 'No!' back and forth, for a whole 24 hours.

I called friends for advice on Monday and Tuesday. All of them said, 'Duh, ride!'

Most of the race was mental. I knew we'd be riding a pace that would have us finishing close to 24 hours after we started. When you know you'll be riding for 24 hours, your mind and body focus on that.

I mentally divided up the race into 3 LD (Limited Distance) rides – 48–56km (30–35 miles) each between the two hour-long vet checks – and I only thought about each mile as it came, each hill climb or canyon as it came, and never thought any further than the vet check ahead of me.

I was a bit surprised at the miles and miles – and miles – of cliffs we rode alongside ... cliffs with drops of 150–300m (500–1000 feet) right beside the 60cm (2-foot) wide path we trotted along. I don't tend to be afraid of heights, and there was nothing to do anyway but keep moving fast along the trail, but there sure are an awful lot of cliffs on that trail. Horses and people have fallen off them. There were also an awful lot of cliffs we rode along that I didn't even see in the dark – and I am glad I never knew or saw them!

I thought we were flying along so fast the whole ride, and yet we were continually up against the time cut-offs at the vet checks. (There are two-hour holds and a number of vet checks that you have to stay at, so you don't want to waste time there.) That was always something of a worry dogging us the whole ride, adding a bit of stress. We actually finished with just 19 minutes to spare, and on the very last stretch, not knowing exactly how far we had to go to get to the finish, the last 30 minutes or so were pretty nerve-racking!

The whole thing was just magical, perfect – how the opportunity unexpectedly materialised; that I rode such a strong, amazing horse; that I finished my first Tevis. It was just meant to be. I can't put in words how thrilled I was to complete the Tevis. (Yes, I cried at the finish when Quinn passed his final vet check!) I was astounded at the effort made by him, and utterly grateful to him for the ride of a lifetime. And the fact that my friend Nance just gave me her horse to ride is ... it's just beyond what a good friend would do for someone.

Now when I pick up and hold my silver Tevis buckle in my hands, and when I put it on, I can still scarcely believe I got to do it. It has to be one of my proudest accomplishments!

Merri Melde completed the Tevis Cup in 2009. For more information, visit TheEquestrianVagabond.com

Type Foot
Date Year-round
Distance As far as possible in 24 hours
Main obstacles Mental
Website iau-ultramarathon.org
They call it 'What gives life its value, if not its constant
cry, for self-transcendence?' – Sri Chinmoy

Competitors say
❝One lives one lifetime during a
marathon but one lives through
several lifetimes in a 24-hour race.❞

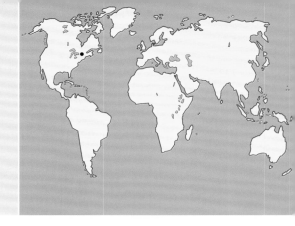

24-Hour Track Race

Round and round and round again. Is this the ultimate test of physical and mental strength? 24 hours, one 400m (440-yard) running track and no predefined distance: the only goal is to go as far and as hard as possible ... and not get bored!

Track sessions might be tough, but they are an integral part of any serious runner's training regimen. However, it doesn't matter how hard a track session an athlete is preparing for, nothing can quite compare to the 24-hour track race. Just imagine setting off on the start of a 400m (440-yard) athletics track and running in 'circles' for the next 24 hours. That's it. Your goal is to cover as much ground as possible in those 24 hours (and not collapse in the process). To run 160km (100 miles), you will have completed 400 laps. But you probably won't have won the race.

The distances covered in these events are staggering. The World Record for a 24-hour track event is held by Yiannis Kouros, a Greek who ran 304km (188.59 miles) in 1997 during the Sri Chinmoy Ultra Festival in Adelaide, Australia. The women's record is held by Mami Kudo of Japan, who ran 254km (158.126 miles) in Taipei, Taiwan in December 2009. As a general guide, anything over 160km (100 miles) is seen as a milestone for the challenge – an average of over 6km/h (4 mph) or over 16 laps every hour for 24 hours.

Unlike the majority of the races in this book, the 24-hour track race is not confined to a particular country, city or region. There are numerous races around the world. As such, temperature and climate will vary between races, and those in hotter climes may be tougher than those in cooler areas. But the ethos remains the same: an official outdoor (or indoor) running track is the regulated 400m (440 yards) the world over and is obviously laid flat. As such, any venue anywhere can potentially offer this quite unique challenge.

And it is an incredible feat of physical strength. Of course, unlike some of the ultra-distance races in the world, athletes do not have to tackle difficult terrain or deal with aggressive ascents or descents. Instead, they simply have to keep going. And therein lies the challenge. The physicality of the race is beyond doubt: the strain it places on the lower body and arms is immense. What's more, running so many laps in either direction (often, this changes at regular intervals) puts incredible sustained pressure on the inner leg.

right A 24-hour track race can occur anywhere in the world, wherever there is the standard 400m (440-yard) athletics track

But perhaps tougher than the physical challenge is the mental. It may sound obvious, but the strain of seeing the same surrounds, the same landmarks and the same bends over and over again can take an immense toll on a tired mind. Many ultra-distance runners refer to the importance of being able to look at the scenery as they run; it offers them a mental escape of sorts. There is no such liberty on a 24-hour track race. Instead, it is the competitor against their mind. If the fatigue or boredom of the mind defeats them, then they are out. Only the most single-minded, obstinate athlete will be able to keep going for the full 24 hours.

During the race, athletes are allowed to enlist the assistance of support teams to keep them motivated – and more importantly fuelled – while they run. If no supporters are forthcoming, most races allow an athlete to pitch a tent by the side of a track that will contain provisions and an area for an albeit short rest. In fact, as far as ultra-distance races go, this is one that requires very little equipment: athletes need little more than a pair of running shoes, running gear and the provisions to keep them fuelled.

Most ultra-distance runners go beyond the physical when it comes to the pursuit of their sport. They spend hours and hours pushing themselves mentally and physically to go further and faster than they have before. One of the major organisers of 24-hour track races and running races around the world is the Sri Chinmoy marathon team,

above The track becomes the runner's entire world

above and right One of the most famous events is the annual Ottawa 24-Hour Track Race

which is centred on this spiritual aspect to running. Founded upon the philosophies of spiritual teacher, poet, artist and athlete Sri Chinmoy, the goal is to realise self-transcendence and self-improvement through physical fitness. Under the Sri Chinmoy philosophy, competitors in these races do not compete against others, only themselves and their past results. As such, every competitor is deemed a winner.

To complete this race, and go as far as they can, an athlete needs to be able to tap into the spiritual aspect of what they do. Achieving this state will allow competitors to tackle the extreme mental and physical strains placed on the body by what must be one of the most repetitive – and challenging – running events in existence.

Nadeem Khan

Training incorporates an equal preparation between the mental and physical aspects of the race. In my years as a 24-hour runner I found the physical training a lot easier than the mental preparation. The physical training is tangible; it, at least, is easily seen.

When I was running 24-hour races competitively, I used to average about 96–110km (60–70 miles) per week, including two long runs. To prepare mentally, I liked to run my race in my mind prior to going through it. I have held on to the same strategy throughout my running career, up to my international career on the Canadian national team.

The biggest obstacle in preparation for a 24-hour race is 'not knowing the unknown'. When I ran shorter distances, I ran close to or past the race distance. However, with 24 hours it is not physically possible without overstressing oneself. It is also hard to get your body used to running at night, when it wants to go to sleep.

The secret to a good 24-hour race is to divide it into different sections. From taking every 5km (3 miles) at a time to dividing up the race into 10-minute segments. The 24-hour race is a good metaphor for life. We do not plan everything we are going to do in life at one shot. We also change our goals as we move along life. The same is true of a 24-hour run. One lives one lifetime during a marathon, but one lives through several lifetimes in a 24-hour race.

Ultimately, a 24-hour run is not an easy challenge. To stay awake for that kind of time frame is difficult enough, but to add physical exercise to the equation is not an easy task. It is not only a race with the others but also a race against yourself. The arms start hurting from the constant back and forth motion around the 12-hour mark, the legs start cramping at about the 18-hour mark and the mind starts getting tired at the 20-hour mark.

I, personally, do not experiment with my nutrition and hydration during the race. It is important to realise that different foods come into play at different times of the day. I start with semi-solid foods at the start; in the evenings (about 10 hours into the race) I start taking some solid foods, and lots of soup and warm beverages at night.

The last hour of the race is the most amazing. Everyone on the track is going through the same motions and enduring the same feelings. But to be out and about in the last hour is the finale on a day's accomplishment. After the completion of the 24 hours, the feeling of pain and tiredness gives way to a feeling of elation and a sense of accomplishment.

Nadeem Khan has run seven 24-hour races, four of which have been on a running track (including Ottawa).

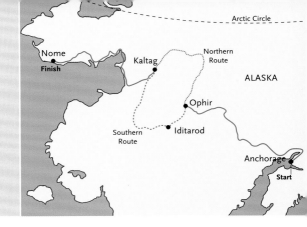

Type Dogsled
Date March
Distance Varies, but average 1850km (1150 miles)
Main obstacles Terrain, cold
Website www.iditarod.com
They Call It The Last Great Race on Earth

Competitors say
❝At the time it was really painful but what was I going to do, just stop? I had to keep trying.❞

Iditarod

One musher, sixteen dogs and over 1600km (1000 miles) of Alaskan wilderness, the Iditarod is a gruelling test of human – and animal – endurance. Teams (musher and dogs) tackle an age-old trail that is all-too-often hidden from view by whiteout conditions, overcoming temperatures that can fall to –46°C (–51°F), winds that hit 80km/h (50mph), and the very real threat of death. There's a reason why the whole of Alaska stops on the first Saturday in March to celebrate the start of one of the great wilderness races.

below The race is the highlight of the Alaskan dogsled calendar.

At the end of the 19th century, settlers hungry for gold descended on Alaska in their thousands. They struck north, crossing the wilderness on steamships in the summer, and occasionally (if they dared tackle the harsh conditions) by dogsleds on the Iditarod trail in the winter. But as the gold dried up and airplanes replaced the dogsleds, the trail all but disappeared, remembered only in history books and local folklore.

That was until 1964, when Dorothy G. Page decided something should be done to celebrate the endeavours of those who had lived, thrived and died on the Iditarod trail. Talk turned into action, and in 1967 a 40km (25-mile) race was launched with 58 mushers vying for a share of $25,000. While Page's original goal had been to end the race in Iditarod, a couple of school teachers thought about taking it further – 1600km (1000 miles) further in fact to a Bering Sea outpost called Nome. Gelo Huyck and Tom Johnson set about organising a race – and offering a $51,000 prize purse to boot. In 1973 the Iditarod was born.

In 1973, 33 mushers started out and 22 of them finished. Dick Wilmarth won the race in 20 days, 48 minutes and 41 seconds. Despite the lack of a prize purse in 1974, the race went ahead with 44 mushers, and in 1975 the organisers secured corporate

sponsorship and thus the future of one of the toughest events on the planet.

Today's Iditarod is an entirely different beast from the one that Huyck and Johnson (not to mention Page) envisaged. An international endurance challenge that pitches mushers – many of whom are household names in the frozen north – against the best that Mother Nature can throw at them in one of the most inhospitable places on earth.

Temperatures can easily plummet to –46°C (–51°F), the wind whips through the barren interior at up to 80km/h (50mph) (leading to a total whiteout and also blowing snow across the trails and hiding any markers), and wind chill has been measured as low as –90°C (–130°F). Mushers have been known to lose fingers to frostbite, disappear for days at a time, and plummet through ice bridges into horrifically cold water. Sleds also have to tackle local wildlife, and many dogs have been killed by rampaging moose during the course of the race. Needless to say, when things go wrong there isn't a lot of help in the wilderness.

But the teams have to get to the wilderness first. And in a lot of respects, that is the easy bit. The race starts in Anchorage to massive fanfare, with parts of the city shut down and spectators turning out in their thousands to watch the sleds head towards the first checkpoint. The first team – an honorary choice based on their services to sledding – leaves at 10 a.m., and then after that teams leave every two minutes.

This first portion of the race is largely ceremonial. Mushers auction spots on the sled to help pay for the cost of assembling the teams and are followed by thousands of fans.

It's after Checkpoint Two that the real fun begins. After 160km (100 miles) of flat (known as Moose alley), the trail climbs up the Rainy Pass to an elevation of 980m (3215 feet), and Mother Nature starts to have her fun. This part of the trail is where the wind whips and the temperatures fall. Only then do the teams face the most hazardous segment of the race. Dropping in to Dalzell Gorge, the ice-packed trail descends 300m (984 feet) in just 8km (5 miles), making conditions treacherous for both the dogs and their mushers. From there, the trail winds its way north. In odd-numbered years, the trail follows a southern route, taking in the ghost town of Iditarod. In even numbered years it loops around to the north.

Once the trails re-merge at Kaltag, the teams begin a 483km (300-mile) race for Nome. With enforced stoppages (to protect both the dogs and the drivers), this last dash is a true test of both nerve and mettle. And it really is a race, with teams often separated by mere hours. In fact, in 1978 Dick Mackey and Rick Swenson were separated by just one second (the noses of Mackey's lead dogs, Skipper and Shrew, sealed the victory). In 2011, John Baker broke the course record, crossing the line in 8 days, 19 hours and 46 minutes.

The Iditarod is a return to the heart and soul of the wilderness. To complete it – let alone win – a musher must motivate themselves through long stints of sleep-deprived night-time sledding when the temperature plummets and the wind whistles through the lonely Alaskan interior, and must manage and care for his team of dogs too. Sixteen dogs start the race on a team, six have to finish. It is a team race, and every single member of that team – man and dog – cross that line knowing they have faced up to Mother Nature, and she let them pass.

Aliy Zirkle

ATHLETE PERSPECTIVE

The Iditarod for me is more than a race. It takes 365 days per year of my life to prepare myself and my dogs. In that respect, it's a lifestyle. If you want to be successful, then it is an all-encompassing endeavour.

To be ready for the race, you have to get a few different parts right. The part that most people see is the physical fitness aspect of getting ready to run 1600km (1000 miles) in eight-and-a-half to ten days. The physical aspect is both human and canine. I don't think that you can underestimate the human aspect of being able to get out in the Arctic at temperatures as low as –30°C (–22°F). Not only that, but being physically able to make it 1600km (1000 miles) and be the coach, the caretaker and the sled driver for the dogs who are basically pulling you.

Just as important as the physical is the mental. You have to be prepared for the fact that you are travelling across the wilderness. When we say we go from one village in Alaska to another village, that could be a village where its heyday was in 1910 and now two people live there. So you have to be able to support yourself and your dogs at all times. Mentally, that's a hurdle that most people don't realise until they get out on a race. It's hard to train for that.

And you never know what is going to happen. I've been charged by a buffalo; I took a wrong turn on the pack ice of the frozen ocean and ended up coming across an open lead (that, thank goodness, stopped); my headlights blew out and I didn't have a headlight for about 24 hours (and there isn't much daylight up here). All these scenarios are things that you have to be mentally prepared to deal with.

The other part of the Iditarod that I haven't mentioned is the competitive part of it. You get physically and mentally ready to go 1600km (1000 miles), but you could just go and camp and do that. You're supposed to do this race faster than anyone else, and that part about it is total focus on yourself and your team when you're out there so you know what's going on and what are your limitations. But you have to have some peripheral vision so you can see what other teams are doing, what the trail conditions are doing, what the weather is doing. You take all this into account and it's like you're putting yourself into a chess game: the move you make will be countered by the other teams. That's the part about it that makes it more intriguing.

You have to be cautious about knowing your dogs, knowing your individuals and knowing yourself and be able to push your teams to a point – not too far – where you can win.

Aliy Zirkle has completed the Iditarod for 12 consecutive years, coming second in 2012. She has competed in numerous dogsled races and was the first – and only – woman to win the Yukon Quest. You can find out more information at: spkenneldoglog.blogspot.com.

Type Foot, ski or bike
Date February
Distance 160, 480 or 690km (100, 300 or 430 miles)
Main obstacles Cold, distance, mental
Website www.arcticultra.de
They call it The world's coldest and toughest ultra

Competitors say
❝ *Everything about the Yukon Arctic Ultra is tough: the distance, terrain, cold, loneliness ... the list goes on.* ❞

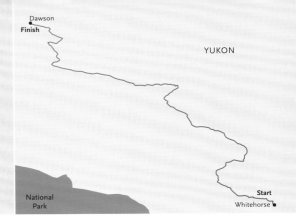

Dawson
Finish
YUKON
National Park
Start
Whitehorse

Yukon Arctic Ultra

A supreme test not only of endurance but of survival as well. The Yukon Arctic Ultra pushes athletes further and harder than they've ever gone before.

The winter in Northern Canada is harsh. Temperatures can plummet to −50°C (−58°F), the wind can blow at −30°C (−22°F) and the sun, when it makes an appearance, does little to warm the bones. Only the hardiest individuals stay in the frozen north, braving up to six months of snow and wind in some truly inhospitable conditions. Inhospitable but

spectacular, because while the weather might be deadly, the surrounds are incredible. From the aurora borealis to snow kissed mountains, frozen lakes and ice-bound forests, Canada in the winter is stunning.

And it is against this backdrop that athletes tackle the Yukon Arctic Ultra. Undoubtedly one of – perhaps even the

right The race is a test of endurance and survival

– coldest ultra-distance races on the planet, the Yukon Arctic Ultra is a test not only of endurance but of survival as well. This is a self-supported race along the legendary route of the Yukon Quest Trail. Of course, there are checkpoints along the route where athletes are given warm food and drinks, shelter and any medical assistance that is required. What's more, race stewards patrol the route on skidoos. But most athletes will see these stewards only once in a 24-hour period, and the checkpoints can be as much as a day apart from one another. And so it is essential that every athlete – regardless of the discipline – has everything they need to maintain forward momentum, and survive, when things get tough.

This they do before the gun even goes off: to stand any chance of completing this race, every competitor has to understand and manage their body's reaction to the cold. Standing around waiting for the gun in temperatures that can range from −18°C to −50°C (0°F to −58°F), with added wind chill as low as −25°C (−13°F), places a huge strain on the body. But it doesn't get any easier once the athletes start moving. As the body heats up, the athletes start to sweat, creating a fine layer of perspiration on the surface of their skin, which can then freeze.

As such, it is essential that all athletes carry the right equipment and maintain it properly. As you might imagine,

or catch a few restless hours of sleep at a checkpoint. Most competitors talk about hallucinations during the race, and many are forced out of the race because of the tricks that the lack of sleep and relentless cold are playing on their bodies and minds.

Competitors have three choices when tackling the Yukon Arctic Ultra: foot, ski or bike. All present their own unique challenges and some, obviously, take longer than others. But all share the common need to follow the trail through both day and night. For the most part it is marked clearly. However, the weather conditions change rapidly in this part of the world and trail markers can easily get buried beneath fresh snowfall. As such, all athletes need to have a semblance of navigation skill and be prepared to find their way back on course should they take a wrong turn.

Needless to say, not everyone who starts the race finishes it (around 30 per cent of competitors fail to finish

below A spectacular start to a truly gruelling test

the list of mandatory equipment to be carried in a race like this ranges from what is needed to maintain a level of comfort, and what is needed simply to survive. Even the basics become a struggle, with water freezing at these temperatures and containers breaking as a result. What's more, carrying this equipment is no mean feat, and many competitors choose to use pulks (sledges) to drag their kit along.

But perhaps the toughest part of the race is the lack of sleep (especially when coupled with the relentless cold). To ensure that they pass the checkpoints before the cut-off times, athletes have little opportunity to rest along the way. When they do rest, it is often to bivvy on the side of the trail over all disciplines and distances). Athletes tackling the 160km (100-mile) race have the option to extend to 480km (300 miles) if they feel fit and medical officers pass them as so. The 690km (430-mile) race is a different beast altogether and is run only every other year. Footrace competitors in this discipline can expect to spend anything up to 300 hours on the trail, with the winner completing it in just over 200 hours (only four of the 15 footrace starters finished the race in 2011). At the time of writing, no cross-country skiers have managed to complete the 690km (430-mile) event, and only three mountain bikers have done so (Brit Alan Sheldon holds the record in 99 hours, 30 minutes).

The Yukon Arctic Ultra is tough. The confluence of cold, sleep deprivation, harsh trail conditions and relentless physical demands place enormous strain on the competitors who tackle the race. Many fail to make it to the finish. However, those who do know that they have completed one of the world's toughest challenges in some of the harshest environmental conditions.

Dave Berridge

ATHLETE PERSPECTIVE

I had raced in the Yukon Arctic Ultra twice before. First the 160km (100-mile) distance – I did it as an introductory course to see if I could race in the Arctic. Having raced predominately in the heat (deserts and jungles), I was curious to see if I could.

With lessons learnt and the satisfaction of reaching the finish line of what I considered to be my hardest 160km (100 miles), the same old curiosity was stirred to see if I could do the 480km (300 miles).

The following year, that curiosity was satisfied: I could. The lessons I had learnt about pace, clothing, equipment, sleep management, how to pack a sled, keep liquid from freezing and what to eat whilst moving, proved to be invaluable. In effect, I had served my apprenticeship.

So the lessons learnt during those two races were key. Also I spent the previous 12 months training and racing. I raced regularly in things as small as the New Forest 10 to the Norseman Extreme Triathlon, culminating in the Kalahari Augrabies Extreme Marathon some 14 weeks before the start of the YAU. I was basically trying to get 'match fit'.

The mental preparation is a complicated and personal process. Basically the key is visualisation! By that, I mean contemplating the route, trail conditions likely to be encountered, obstacles that may or may not appear.

Every worst-case scenario was solved in my head before reaching the start line.

An example of this was that my sled broke. It was a break that I had seen happen to another racer a couple of years ago, so I worked out how to fix it, should the same thing happen to me. Needless to say, it happened and it took less than 10 minutes to stop and fix. I didn't have to think about how to fix it, as I already knew and I had immediate access to my repair kit.

My motivation during the race was driven by a fear of failure and fear of getting caught. I've thought about this a lot. Why do some people fail to finish and others don't? Ego, pride, stubbornness, vanity, determination ... I still don't know the answer. In the end I simply wanted – no had – to reach Dawson, absolutely nothing else mattered.

Of course, I faced issues on the way: frost-bitten feet and an ear – two stupid mistakes that both happened near the end and because of lack of sleep. I left my shoes outside my sleeping bag during the last bivvy and they froze; and my ear because when I was approaching Dawson the race organiser came out to meet me and give directions to the finish line. I lifted my hat and goggles and hadn't realised I hadn't covered my one ear. Two silly mistakes.

When I reached Dawson ... wow! My first reaction was relief: I had done it. Only when I realised that out of the 20 starters only four of us made it did I begin to appreciate the achievement. Everything about the Yukon Arctic Ultra is tough: the distance, the terrain, the cold, the loneliness, the isolation ... the list goes on. But what a race and what a place! If you can appreciate where you are and how lucky you are to be there, it helps – it might only help a little, but it helps.

Dave Berridge has completed the Yukon Arctic Ultra on three occasions, finishing the 160, 480 and 690km (100-, 300- and 430-mile) races.

Type Dogsled
Date February
Distance 1600km (1000 miles)
Main obstacles Cold, terrain, distance
Website www.yukonquest.com
They call it An epic winter sports event

Competitors say
❝It's just as much a survival race as it is a competitive race.❞

Yukon Quest

Fourteen canine athletes and one musher – that is how it is described. But, in reality, 15 athletes start the Yukon Quest, a historic dash across the Canadian and Alaskan wilderness in search of one of the ultimate prizes in dogsledding.

below It's a lonely but spectacular race

Breath that freezes as soon as it is exhaled. The crunch of fresh snow underfoot. The distant howl of wild wolves. The spirit of the Yukon – the spirit of Northern Canada – is characterised by a raw splendour. And it is against this splendour that the Yukon Quest is run.

However, the origins of this great race – perhaps rivalled only by the Iditarod on the dogsled calendar – are a little more whimsical. They involve beer, a late night and four mushers with an idea. That idea was to run the ultimate dogsled race. It would take place along the historic route of the Yukon River – a one-time highway for those seeking their fortune in the gold fields of the Klondike. On that legendary night back in 1983, Roger Williams, Leroy Shank, Ron Rosser

and Willie Libb had no idea that they were on the cusp of creating an endurance race of international repute. That's exactly what they did. Twenty-six teams took part in the first Yukon Quest in 1984. Twenty finished over the course of 16 days, with Sonny Lindner taking the inaugural title in just over 12 days. Now, things are slightly different.

But not everything. The spirit and motivation that brought together the race still holds true. At its heart, the Yukon Quest is about the athletes. It is about the tradition and history of a remarkable part of North America. And it is about the challenge.

A challenge that takes the teams across four mountain ranges – the highest point on the course being the 1220m (4002-foot) King Solomon's Dome – along frozen rivers, and through isolated outposts. What's more, all of this takes place in temperatures that have been known to hit –65°C (–85°F) and against winds that can whip along the course at 160km/h (100mph). Each year, the course goes back on itself, meaning that the teams travel from Whitehorse in the Yukon to Fairbanks, Alaska one year, and back the other way the next. This gives every musher the opportunity to 'go and return' along this historic route.

But to make it to the start line the musher has to assemble, master, and care for a team of 14 huskies. The dogs are bred for the purpose of running, and the preparation of these teams is probably the most important consideration for any musher attempting to complete the race. Teams are chosen with care, with dogs weighing anything up to 30kg (80lb) selected to take part. Every aspect of the dog is looked at and managed, from the way that they eat to the structure of their feet. Why? Because when fatigued, a pernickety eater will become more pernickety, or a dog that has spaced-out toes could struggle on the trail and so hinder its performance. Needless to say, with a considerable prize purse up for grabs, each musher is searching for consistency and strength.

And that is why they run the race to suit their teams. Dogs sweat only through the mouth and feet, and so if it is a warm year, most of the race will be run at night. Along each stage, teams will typically run and rest for an even amount of time (five hours running, five hours resting). And during that downtime, the musher will ensure the dogs are rested, fed and cared for. So even though the dogs do much of the physical work, the mushers have a constant task for the duration of the quest.

It's a race that, at over 1600km (1000 miles) in length, is itself relentless. The length between checkpoints varies from 53 to 160km (33–100 miles) and so mushers are frequently forced to camp out on the trail. During the race, there is one compulsory stop – 36 hours in Klondike – to give mushers the opportunity to rest and allow vets to examine the animals. But for the most part this is a battle of attrition. Of course, the animals are frequently examined during the race, and stores are laid in advance with the food that each musher requires for his or her team. But once in the wilderness if anything serious goes wrong, the musher has to be ready to act until help can arrive.

Against a challenging background, the race is run at a remarkable speed. Hans Gatt holds the course record: 9 days, 26 minutes. At the back – and there are prizes for last place – teams can take anything up to 16 days to complete the gruelling course.

The Yukon Quest is a true battle of man and beast against the elements. Yes, the huskies work tirelessly to transport the musher and equipment to the finish line. But the musher also works tirelessly – and with the utmost care – to ensure that they can do just that. It is a team event, and the team that works best together inevitably wins it; and survives the challenges of one of the remotest parts of North America.

Brent Sass

ATHLETE PERSPECTIVE

I live, eat and breathe my sled dogs – it's kind of a lifestyle. I live in a remote place in Alaska where we raise and train the dogs in order to be able to go out and race. To be successful in the Quest it's all about exposing yourself to as much as you can. In the Yukon Quest you face temperatures of –65°C to –55°C (–85 to –67°F) with winds of 65km/h (40mph) and snowstorms. Up here I get all that and I train with the dogs in those conditions so that we are prepared when we get to the race.

But I think more than anything the Yukon Quest is mental. The mental challenges are the biggest things you have to overcome out there. There are so many challenges that you have to prepare for physically. But mentally, when it's –45°C (–49°F) and the wind is blowing and you're in the middle of nowhere and you have no support and nothing else but you and your dogs and the stuff you have in your sled, you have to be mentally strong. If you are strong mentally, then you can get through anything.

It's also about knowing how to survive in those cold temperatures and remote places. That's the thing about the Yukon Quest: you travel through some of the most remote places in North America and it's really important that you're comfortable being in those places with your dogs.

To be a good musher you need to have the mental attitude, the focus and the ability to overcome the challenges. We face a lot out there and those challenges can be anything from things happening to yourself – you might get frostbite in your finger or nose, or if your feet are frozen – all the way down to those 14 dogs you are running. You have to watch their feet, their possible injuries and their frostbite. You have to be watching all of that while at the same time trying to take care of yourself and, at the same time as that, trying to race. It's just as much a survival race as it is a competitive race. For those in their rookie year, it is about survival. For those of us competing and going for the win, we have to have all of that taken care of so we can focus on being fast on the trail.

When things get hard, my dogs keep me going. The thing I like most about mushing is the bond and the connection we build with dogs. The bigger the bond you have, the further they will go and the more effort they will put in. So when you're in those treacherous times in the race and you're starting to feel down, it's the dogs I turn to. It's the same with the dogs. If I have a positive attitude through this thing, then the dogs stay positive and they can power through the bad conditions. And I love the wilderness, I love being alone with my dogs and I love the challenge. The challenge really drives me. When I go out there and its –40°C (–40°F) below and my fingers, toes and face are frozen and we're moving along the trail, I like that challenge and I take it as something to overcome, and between me and the dogs we can do that.

Brent Sass has raced the Yukon Quest six times, finishing as high as fourth in 2011. For more information on Brent, visit wildandfreealaska.com

Type Foot
Date July
Distance 217km (135miles)
Main obstacles Heat, distance, elevation change
Website www.badwater.com
They call it The world's toughest footrace.

Competitors say
It makes you pull effort out from the deepest parts of your body and challenges your mind at the highest level.

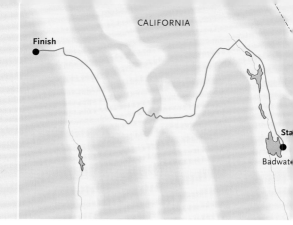

CALIFORNIA

Finish

Sta

Badwat

Badwater Ultramarathon

A relentless sun, an uphill course and 217km (135 miles) of running through the salt flats of Death Valley, the Badwater Ultramarathon is a test not only of physical endurance but mental determination too.

right Nutrition and hydration management are essential

opposite A challenge shared is a challenge halved ... sometimes

There is a reason why the Badwater Ultramarathon proudly carries the moniker of being the world's toughest footrace. Competitors are faced with a 217km (135-mile) route that starts at 85m (280 feet) below sea level in California's Death Valley, and finishes at 2548m (8360 feet) above sea level at Whitney Portal, the trail head to Mount Whitney (a cumulative ascent of 3962m/13,000 feet). The race is also run in July, one of the hottest months in one of the world's most inhospitable regions. As such, it is not uncommon for the mercury to push 49°C (120°F) in an environment where shade is scant and the air oppressively dry.

These are the conditions that impressed Al Arnold in 1973 when he heard about Paxton Beale and Ken Crutchlow completing a 242km (150-mile) relay run from Badwater – the lowest point in the Western Hemisphere – all the way to the top of Mount Whitney – the highest point in the contiguous United States. Inspired by this feat, Arnold decided to try the distance as a solo effort. His first two attempts at the run failed after just 29km (18 miles) on the first go (when his partner collapsed) and 58km (36 miles) on the second (after swelling in his knee prevented him from continuing).

Not to be defeated, however, Arnold embarked on two years of hard training – including hours of cycling in a sauna – and in 1977 the American proved that it really is third time lucky. It took him 84 hours and he lost 8 per cent of his total bodyweight, but Arnold did make it to the top of Mount Whitney, completing the first chapter in the history of the now legendary Badwater Ultramarathon.

Over the next few years, several other ultra runners completed the iconic course, before 1987 became the first year of a head-to-head competitive race. Local regulations meant that a slight route change had to be enforced in 1990, with the official finish line of the race being moved from the summit of the mountain to Whitney Portal (the trailhead to Mount Whitney). Needless to say, these days there are a number of hardy runners who carry on beyond the official finish line in an attempt to 'bag' the summit – and so complete the original route. Of course, there are always those who want to go further, and some athletes opt to run the double, triple or even quad Badwater (there and back twice).

above A lonely, brutal environment

opposite Support teams are vital to competitors

The record for that incredible feat was set by Marshall Ulrich in 2001, in 10 days and 13 hours.

But for most people, the predefined course is enough. And despite the challenges faced en route, the Badwater record books are impressive. For the men, the record stands at 22 hours, 51 minutes and 29 seconds; for the women, 26 hours, 16 minutes and 12 seconds.

To ensure the quality of the 100 athletes invited to participate, the organisers have introduced a 28-hour cut-off at the Panamint Springs Resort checkpoint, and a 48-hour cut-off at the finish line. But to hit those cut-offs you have to get to the start, and that is a tough proposition in itself. Invitations are issued only following the race panel's review of each applicant's endurance credentials. Even before this

review process, applicants must meet at least one of the three minimum qualifying standards, which includes having completed at least three 160km (100-mile) races already.

Once a starting spot is secured, training presents its own challenges. Getting acclimatised to race-day conditions can be of particular difficulty. Pam Reed, who has won the race outright twice, trained at her Arizona base four times a day for between 45 minutes and 1 hour in temperatures as high as 40°C (105°F). Ferg Hawke from Canada, a two-time Badwater runner-up, built a solarium in his back garden and put a treadmill in it to simulate running in temperatures up to 54°C (130°F).

On race day itself, athletes have to provide their own support crew. This team is integral to a successful attempt

at the race, providing all of the necessary nutrition, hydration, massages and other aspects of physical management to ensure their athlete completes the course.

Make it to the end, and what do you receive? Nothing more than a medal and a belt buckle (if you complete in under the 48 hours). However, not many prizes are invested with such effort or push the body to such limits to achieve.

It is clear why the Badwater Ultramarathon really is one of the greatest physical endurance events in the world today.

Jen Segger

ATHLETE PERSPECTIVE

I geared six months of training specifically to this race and to this course. Being a multi-sport athlete, this was a huge mental challenge for me, as I knew that in order to perform to my absolute best, I would have to pull out of other races I wanted to do. My life was pretty much training, eating, sleeping and working. As the volume increased, I was up at 5 a.m. nearly every day to get the workouts in. I was so focused on this race.

Thinking back, I have no idea where the time went and what I did to occupy my mind during these 7-hour runs. The goal was always to get myself into a state of flow, one where time passed by and the mind went numb. That was the sign of a good run! I stayed focused on my game plan for the race, the pace I was going to run. I knew that it was going to hurt, that I would have extreme highs and lows but that I would just push through. I'd walk when I couldn't run. The pain would be temporary.

During the race, I relied on my crew for motivation and support. They kept my pace and kept the atmosphere positive. I was surrounded by my good friends. In fact, I turned my brain completely off and gave all controls to my friend and head of my crew, Ray Zahab. I told him from the beginning that he was to set the tone for me, that I would do as he said. All I wanted to do was run and not have to think. I knew I was in good hands. It was amazing that it took five people to get one person through this race. As I ran and when things got tough, I told myself that I was completing the dream with each step. I had my eyes on Badwater for many, many years and to finally be in the moment, just doing it, you have to embrace it! It's an emotional race on so many levels. It makes you pull effort out from the deepest parts of your body and challenges your mind at the highest level.

At approximately 160km (100 miles) I could see Lone Pine in the distance – somewhere down the road. I was, in fact, on a downhill, but it didn't feel that way. It was midday; the sun was out and I was in full throttle. I remember hitting a tiny dip in the road, something that on any other day a runner wouldn't even notice. I went from feeling great to suddenly an instant feeling of panic, something wasn't right. I was overheating, and very fast. Luckily my crew was right there when this happened. I went over to the van, they took one look at me and then pulled out the special 'body bag cooler' that we carried for this very reason. I was submerged in it instantly to cool my core down. I downed 3l (5 pints) of fluids, and within 15 minutes I was back out and running as if nothing had happened. This is what happens at Badwater. It's a constant struggle between heat balance and how hard you can push!

Badwater to this day is a great memory. Two years after, I drove through Death Valley and it was almost surreal. It was beautiful and it was funny how I could remember every single section of the course! I will be back to run it again, it's unfinished for me. I'm unhappy about how I raced the final climb to the Whitney Portals; I need to go back and overcome that. However, being the youngest female ever on this course, I was happy with a 5th place finish, 9th overall.

Jen Segger is an ultra-endurance athlete. In 2008 Jen finished in ninth place overall at Badwater and was the fifth woman across the line. For more information, visit www.jensegger.com.

Type Bike
Date October
Distance 817km (508 miles)
Main obstacles Distance, heat, elevation change
Website www.the508.com
They call it The toughest 48 hours in sport.

Competitors say
It was the most amazing thing I have ever done in all of my life. It has given me a different view on what my body is capable of.

Furnace Creek 508

Crossing 10 mountain passes, passing through one of the lowest, driest points on the planet, and all of this over a distance of 817km (508 miles), the Furnace Creek 508 is about as brutal as they come.

below The physical and mental exhaustion can be intense

California is a land of extremes – from the bright lights of Hollywood to sleepy hideaways like Palm Springs, from the churning Pacific to the heights of Mount Whitney. And so it is apt that one of the most brutal cycle races on the planet should be played out among these extremes. The Furnace Creek 508 is a race that takes its competitors to exposed heights and sweltering lows as the course weaves through California.

Starting out in Santa Clarita, not far from LA, the route takes competitors away from the City of Angels and pretty much immediately into the mountains. It starts as it means to go on. Crossing 10 mountain passes, winding through Death Valley and then on to the Mojave Desert, riders have just 48 hours to complete the course. Easy? Throw more than 9000m (30,000 feet) of cumulative vertical climbing in to the mix and you start to see why the race has such a fearsome reputation. In short, it is like doing four mountain stages of the Tour de France in just two days.

Needless to say, not everybody finishes what they started. Up to 40 per cent of competitors drop out of the race – or fail to finish before the 48-hour cut-off point. But when you consider the various factors that are played out along the course you can see why.

There are no hiding places during Furnace Creek. And that includes being part of a pack of cyclists. Sure, there is a parade for the first 8km (5 miles) of the event, where riders get to know one another, but as soon as the climbing begins, the conversation ends. And there's good reason for that. Furnace Creek is, for all intents and purposes, a solo ride. There are no pelotons or groups. Athletes must ride alone for the vast majority of the course, receiving only basic assistance along the way from their designated support team.

But to do that, they have to get up the mountains. And the ascents and descents along the course are nothing short of brutal. With more than 9000m (30,000 feet) of climbing throughout the race (and almost the same in descents), the race is all about keeping the pedals ticking over and grinding out the miles. However, the strength required to do that is immense, and the fatigue it engenders merely makes the skill needed to descend efficiently and effectively more difficult to realise.

This fatigue is exacerbated by the constant change in temperature, from the decidedly chilly on the descent of the mountains at night to the unbearably hot in the depths of Death Valley. Despite the race being run in the California autumn, Death Valley and the Mojave Desert can experience temperatures in excess of 33°C (93°F) on a breathless day.

above Every element
challenges athletes
out on the road

Of course, hit the deserts at night, and it is quite a different story. From extreme heat to bone-chilling cold, this part of the world can lose its heat as quickly as it takes it in. And because there are no official stopping points on the course, athletes frequently find themselves cycling through the dead of night in a rapidly cooling, desolate landscape.

It is no surprise, then, that many competitors comment on the tricks their mind plays on them. The constant physical and mental exertion leads them to complain about hallucinations, particularly as they pass through the desert at night.

And that is why the support crews are so vital. Like the athletes in the race, they work hard to make sure cyclists are properly watered and fed. They provide massages and motivation, and keep the rider going as far and as fast as they possibly can. In this respect, the Furnace Creek 508 is tantamount to a team event. No rider is allowed to tackle the race solo, and for good reason.

Of course, a race of this severity attracts a certain calibre of cyclists, and that calibre tends to be pretty top drawer. The course records for the event are an impressive 27 hours, 15 minutes and 21 seconds for men and 28 hours, 46 minutes and 34 seconds for women. That's an average of nearly 30km/h (19mph) and 28km/h (17.5mph) for each, a truly astonishing sustained period of quality endurance riding. Behind these records, the median finishing time is 36 hours at just over 22km/h (14mph).

And if the cycle alone is not enough for you, the race organiser AdventureCORPS also puts on the Badwater Ultramarathon, and have combined the events to form the Death Valley Cup. That is, both races in one year (not one straight after the other). The record for this is a cumulative time of just over 59 hours – 25 hours, 45 minutes for Badwater and 33 hours 20 minutes for the 508, which is a truly impressive ultra-endurance feat.

From the highest heights to the lowest lows, the Furnace Creek 508 is a brutal test of human endurance. Pushing the fittest cyclists to the physical and mental limit, it truly is one of the crown jewels of endurance sport cycling.

Susan Forsman and Shaun Arora

Susan Forsman: I crewed on three occasions in the past to see what it was like and to learn what kind of things the crew had to go through in order to support a solo rider. For my specific training, it was a year-long preparation to do the best I could. Mentally, I prepared to keep in mind that I was doing it for the fun of it, I was doing it to see if I could do it, and the primary goal was to finish the race even if it meant doing it in 48 hours. Physically, I rode a fixed gear bike all year in 2010, with some occasional gear bike rides. I designed my own programme with cycling and strength-training exercises. I prepared with some of the hardest hills and did some interval training to make sure that I had the muscle power to sustain the inevitable fatigue.

Shaun Arora: More experienced riders tried to tell me miles were not as critical. One friend told me that I don't have to bike 800km (500 miles) in two days to prepare for an 800km (500-mile) ride. Another friend and 508 veteran told me to not do any double centuries after Labor Day! I learned about heart-rate training. Riding fixed, I often push my heart too hard, which triggers my asthma. If I biked to work one day and my heart rate was 150 on average, could my next ride be 140?

SF: Since I did the solo category, I had three crew members who made sure I had food, water and anything I could possibly need for the race. The challenge was worrying that I was fast enough for my crew. I had the most talented crew with me, Barley Forsman, Robert Choi and David Hoag, all three long-distance cyclists who have broken records and who hold high standings in ultra-distance races. In the end, I didn't want to disappoint my crew; you cannot go with that calibre of people to a race and not give them a victory.

SA: The big thing that filled my mind was math. I would often calculate my average time, my arrival time, and how much I would need to increase my average to improve certain targets. I would try to increase my average speed by calculating in how many minutes I need to reach my next target. The math goals, the incremental increases, kept me constantly motivated.

SF: My biggest issue was thinking that my equipment was malfunctioning. At about Mile 350 (560km) or so, I thought my saddle was crooked, so I stopped the van and told them about it. Both Robert and Barley got off the van and looked at the bike, checking for the saddle. They didn't find anything wrong with it, but also didn't have the heart to tell me that it was my body. I had mentally prepared myself to battle the wind, rain and sun, so the only thing that could fail was equipment. I wasn't going to defeat myself.

SA: Gearing my fixie was a major factor in how fast I would be. The 508 course has a lot of big uphills and downhills. What gear do you pick for that? I settled on 68 because my heart was pretty sensitive on high climbs. In hindsight, training my heart at 70 would've been better because I had to pause on several descents.

SF: It was the most amazing thing I have ever done in all of my life. It has given me a different view on what my body is capable of, but most importantly I know that I didn't get there on my own. I did pedal all those miles without ever coasting, but if it wasn't for the crew I don't think that I could have done as well as I did.

SA: I loved the race course and riding with others. Being at the back of the pack in ultra races, it is hard to say that I loved the competition aspect. If I was on a geared bike I would be somewhere in the middle, but I would also not receive the special attention or bragging rights that one earns by doing ultra fixed-gear riding.

Susan Forsman and Shaun Arora have both completed the Furnace 508 on a fixed-gear bike.

Type Foot
Date March
Distance 190 or 560km (120 or 350 miles)
Main obstacles Cold, mental
Website www.6633ultra.com
They call it The toughest, coldest and windiest
   extreme ultra-marathon on the planet.

Competitors say
It's the most amazing challenge that anybody will ever have.

6633 Extreme Winter Ultra Marathon

A race against the clock and a battle with the elements, the 6633 Extreme Winter Ultra Marathon pits the hardiest endurance athletes against the best – and worst – of Mother Nature.

right Competitors need to be self-sufficient

opposite With temperatures below −45°C (−49°F) frostbite is a real concern

The Arctic Circle is a brutal place. The wind whips across a frozen expanse, battering the tiny communities that brave the elements in this harsh environment. Almost entirely isolated from the rest of the world, these communities are reliant on the few roads that exist across the wilderness, connecting them with civilisation. These are the very same roads that competitors in the 6633 Arctic Ultra dare to tread.

A race against the clock, a battle against the elements, not to mention a simple fight for survival, the 6633 challenges the athletes that take her on in every way imaginable. 6633 represents both the latitude and minutes of the Arctic Circle – the legendary 'barrier' between civilisation and the top of the world. At a latitude of 66° 33', competitors in the race cross the Circle en route to the finish line. If they choose to do the 190km (120-mile) route (by no means an easy option), that finish line is in Fort McPherson. For those attempting to go the entire distance, that is just a checkpoint on the way to Tuktoyaktuk, which sits on the edge of the Arctic Ocean in Canada's Northwest Territories.

To make it that far, though, competitors have to overcome a host of challenges. Not least the cold. Because in a race that takes place this far north, the cold dictates everything. Temperatures can easily drop to −45°C (−49°F), and that is before wind chill is factored into the equation. At extreme lows, water freezes almost instantly, making everything from hydration to perspiration a significant issue for the athletes. It also places a massive strain on the body, making equipment choice imperative.

Many of the competitors in the 6633 will struggle to replicate the conditions in the Arctic Circle, and once they are out on the trail it is too late to make a kit change. As such, they have to prepare as meticulously as possible to avoid any potential shortfall in cold-weather kit preparation.

The race itself is almost entirely self-supported. All competitors are expected to carry with them what they need to complete the course, and can receive assistance only from the race organisers en route. That means pulling up to 70kg (155-lb) sledges along the frozen highway, placing yet another potentially unfamiliar strain on an already weary body.

And while the race organisers do their utmost to ensure that everyone remains safe while out on the road, competitors can go for significant stretches of time without seeing another soul. It can be mentally challenging to be alone in a dangerous and barren environment. As such, psychological strength is a key facet for any athlete attempting to complete the race. As is some basic knowledge of how to survive. Not only against the cold and the wind, but in the face of hunger, dehydration and severe sleep deprivation.

As per most ultra-distance races, there are strict time limits placed on competitors throughout the race. To complete the 6633, all athletes must be prepared to spend the majority of the days and nights on their feet, and pretty much all of it without sleep. The sleep monsters (or extreme sleep deprivation) are a very real threat on race day, and competitors have been known to fall asleep while standing

up or to hallucinate while walking along. In most races, this would not be too dangerous. However, in a race like the 6633 there are numerous problems associated with falling asleep in an inhospitable and unsuitable place.

Not least the fact that the race is played out on what is not only a working highway but also (in parts) an airstrip. While this part of the north may feel completely isolated, competitors have to be wary of passing traffic that may not be able to react too quickly to a weary athlete. Admittedly, not too many planes land up there and the juggernauts are largely kept away by the hurricane-force katabatic winds that plague parts of the highway (yet another variable to factor into the successful completion of the race), but the threat is ever-present.

With the challenges involved in a race like this the field is small and not everyone completes. In 2011, only Lowri Morgan (one of six starters) made it all the way to Tuktoyaktuk in 174 hours, 8 minutes. Four of the six starters in the 190km (120-mile) race completed the course. The completion rate isn't much better in previous years, with nobody completing the 560km (350-mile) course in 2010, and only Christopher Todd completing the race in 2009. That is a testament to how tough the challenge really is.

All of the elements combine in the 6633 Arctic Ultra to challenge competitors on every level. It strips them raw both physically and psychologically, and only the truly tough tackle the race – let alone go on to complete it.

Mimi Anderson

The 6633 was the first cold race that I had ever done. So I wrote myself out an action plan about how I was going to tackle it, and I really wasn't sure what to expect. I loved it, but it's tough.

There are a lot of people who go out and don't have a plan – how to tackle it and how long to spend at checkpoints – and that's very easy to do. I planned this race like A, B and C, so I just got on with it. You know you're going to have bad patches, but you talk yourself out of them. You know how you're going to cope, but you also know that because of the situation you are in you can't afford to faff around – you have to remain focused because it could be a situation of life and death if you are stupid. I just get on with it.

In my head I would know that I was going to go 100km (60 miles) to the next checkpoint and I knew that it was going to take me however many hours to do that. (I was quite lucky in that usually I kept within my time references.) From that point of view, I knew what to expect.

However, I didn't know how I was going to cope with the cold – I'm not very good with it and I don't like it. But again, you put yourself in the situation and you have to get on with it. The year that we did it was the coldest year. You had to have every part of your skin covered, otherwise you would be liable to get frostbite. So you wear ski masks and goggles and every time you eat you have to go through this whole process of taking off your mitts, lifting your goggles, getting your food out, pulling your mask down, shoving it down, covering yourself back up, chewing the food – and then you do it again.

Sleep deprivation is the worst issue on top of the cold – it was tough. I didn't mind being on my own – I spent most of the race on my own and I didn't mind that as I was prepared for it. The sleep was tough, though – at about 170km (105 miles) coming to the checkpoint I was found sleeping standing up. I just kept on going and kept on falling asleep and that was the worst bit – the lack of sleep and the hallucinations.

But it is beautiful. It's the most amazing challenge that anybody will ever have. It's much more extreme in my view than running in the heat, and there are so many wow factors there that it is just an adventure. I loved it.

Mimi Anderson is a legend in ultra-running circles. Among her many achievements are becoming the first woman to complete the Double Badwater and a world record for seven days running on a treadmill. For more on Mimi, visit marvellousmimi.com.

Type Multi-discipline | **Date** November
Distance 514km (320 miles)
Main obstacles Heat, currents
Website www.ultramanlive.com
What it takes Individual resources are shared in an atmosphere where everyone can be a winner and the pursuit of human excellence is the fundamental rule.

Competitors say
❝*Although some of the races that I have competed in have been demanding, none of them could be described as the ultimate – that is, until I discovered Ultraman Hawaii.*❞

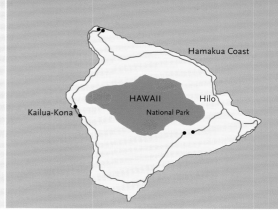

Ultraman World Championships

For many, the thought of an Ironman is hard enough. Those willing to take on the Ultraman are prepared to go nearly three times the distance on one of the world's toughest courses battling heat, wind and the inevitable fatigue.

below The famed lava fields of Oahu

Every year, the eyes of the triathlon world turn to Kona for one of the most famous races on the planet. The Ironman World Championships is one of the most gruelling – and competitive – events on the triathlon calendar. Away from that World Championships, though, the Big Island of Hawaii is home to another race. It's longer, tougher – nearly three times as long, in fact – and takes days to complete. It is the Ultraman World Championships.

Founded in 1983 – just five years after the inaugural Ironman – the Ultraman World Championships pushes a small field of elite athletes to the absolute limits of human endurance over three competitive days of swimming, cycling and running.

To enter, you have to be good – very good, in fact. To be eligible for an invitation, athletes must have either competed in a previous Ultraman World Championships or competed at Ultraman Canada (there are other Ultraman events throughout the world that can also lead to eligibility), and must also have completed an Ironman within 18 months of the race date. Simply finishing one of the 'qualifying' events is tough enough. To be selected after that event, you have to be something special.

A breakdown of the demands placed on the athletes goes some way to explaining why.

The three-day event starts before the sun rises above the ocean at Kailua Pier with a 10km (6-mile) swim to Keahou. In warm waters (touching 21°C/70°F), wetsuits are optional, although organisers do recommend their use due to the profusion of jellyfish in the water. Each swimmer has a designated support crew in the water, who are there to provide them with food and hydration. They are also there to help them when things get tough. And they do. Most notably towards the end of the swim section of the race, where ocean swells and strong currents make swimming difficult, and sharp lava outcrops wait menacingly for those who stray too close to the cliffs. The cut-off for this first portion of the race is 5 hours, 30 minutes and not everyone makes it.

But for those who do, the day isn't over. Immediately after exiting the water, the athletes are faced with a 145km (90-mile) bike. Cycling the Big Island is tough. Cycling it with 10km (6 miles) of swimming under your belt is extraordinary. Athletes begin the cycle through the tremendous heat of the midday sun. This is a heat that rebounds off the lava fields and is whipped along the course by relentless winds. What's more, the bike is pretty much uphill all the way, with cyclists 'enjoying' 2316m (7600 feet) of climbing as they make their way up to the Day One finish point at Namakani Pao – hopefully within the 12-hour cut-off.

Of course, it doesn't get any easier on Day Two. Again

the heat, again the wind and this time 2621m (8600 feet) of climbing over a gruelling 276km (171 miles). Athletes have 12 hours to complete the route from Namakani Paio to the Kohala Village Inn on already weary legs.

And that is all before they start Day Three. A nice and 'easy' 84km (52-mile) double-marathon stroll through the lava fields awaits those who have made it this far. Apart from the distance and already tired legs, the challenge of running in the heat with potentially windy conditions makes this a day that can break even the strongest athletes.

Competition on the course is fierce. The record is held at 21 hours, 41 minutes for men (Holger Spiegel, 2010) and 24

above Hawaii offers a beautifully brutal challenge

hours, 7 minutes for women (Amber Monforte, 1998). But the pedigree of those who compete in the race is enough to ensure that everyone out there is targeting an impressive time.

The Ultraman is unique. Embodying the best in Hawaiian values, it engenders an environment where athletes push themselves way beyond what could be considered 'normal' human endurance. In doing so, they become part of a unique family that shares and understands the values of the islands on which the race is run. What's more, to have the strength and determination to compete a race that places so many demands on the human body means that those who do cross that finish line know they are part of an elite group of endurance competitors.

Amber Monforte

ATHLETE PERSPECTIVE

I've found that the mental aspect is probably the most important. At some point in every athlete's race, there will be a point where it hurts, and it would be so easy to throw in the towel. We all have those moments. Part of why I like doing endurance racing is because it is a challenge mentally and I learn something about myself and how I react under pressure. This does not mean that I don't do the physical training, but I think in ultras the mental toughness is what gets people to the finish line. The long training rides and runs for me are the most enjoyable part about getting ready for UM. I love having an excuse to get to go for a 10-hour bike ride. It always feels like an adventure getting ready in the morning and hopping on the bike with only a rough plan of where I want to ride for the day.

This year (2011), I had more obstacles than last. I seemed to be either sick or injured from May until about six weeks prior to the race. First pneumonia, then giardia, then Achilles tendonitis, and lastly an SI injury. At about six weeks out, I wasn't sure if I'd physically be able to do the race. My sacroiliac joint was out of alignment and I wasn't able to ride the bike at all. I spent two weeks debating whether or not to race. I had already missed most of my training with injury or illness and now time was running out. The trip had already been planned and paid for, so I intended to head to Hawaii and see how I felt the first week. Luckily, after a couple of trips to my chiropractor, I was back in alignment and able to ride again.

Another obstacle is that I work full time as an RN. My work days last from 6.30 in the morning until 7.30 at night. Training on these days usually involves a 3.45 a.m. wake-up before I do a session or two. Often my before-work sessions are my speed workouts on the treadmill because I get a good effort done in a relatively short amount of time.

The race is the fun part and is like a celebration for all the hard work and sacrifices of the year. I get the normal nerves before the race, especially when I'm standing on the start of the 10km (6-mile) swim. It's hard to wrap my mind around swimming to a point that I can't even see. During the race, there are high and low moments. During the lows, I try and figure out what my body needs to feel better. Usually it means I need more calories. I also try and remember how blessed I am to be able to travel to and participate in these events. I work as a nurse, so getting out and riding and running is what I do for fun and it gives balance to my life.

Over the course of any ultra event, issues will come up, and how your race turns out is about how you handle them. Some of these are planned for before the race, but something unexpected always happens. This year I got seasick for the first time ever swimming. About 3km (1.8 miles) into the swim I started throwing up and it lasted through the first hour of the bike. I ended up having a slower swim and taking a couple extra breaks to try and keep some nutrition and fluids down.

Competing in Hawaii is such a treat. I work as a RN, so I see people all the time that aren't able to do what I do, and I feel really blessed to just be able to do sport.

Ultraman is such an amazing event that does more than encompass the three-day race. The whole experience includes getting together before the race with other athletes and their crews. I call it my family reunion that I get to go to every year in Kona. I get to see people that I haven't seen in a year. We usually do some training rides and swims together, and then there is the post-race celebration paddle in the outriggers. There are so many factors that are out of my control that just finishing the race is my goal. It is always nice to have a fast time, though.

Amber Monforte is a multiple Ultraman Champion.

Type Foot
Date June–August
Distance 4989km (3100 miles)
Main obstacles Terrain, mental
Website 3100.srichinmoyraces.org
They call it The longest certified footrace in the world.

Competitors say
You need to establish your own schedule and maintain your peace of mind, competing with yourself to achieve self-transcendence.

Joseph Austin Playground

Self Transcendence 3100 Mile Race

3100 miles (4989km) around a 0.5488-mile (883m) course in just 52 days. The distance is gruelling, the challenge formidable and the goal clear: competitors in the Self-Transcendence 3100 Mile Race are there to relax and focus.

As the first commuters set off on their way to work in the New York borough of Jamaica, Queens, the race begins. The athletes run past the traffic, the school children, the homeless, mothers with pushchairs ... the list is endless. But for 52 days of the year the competitors of the Self Transcendence 3100 Mile race become part of Jamaica. Admittedly, parts of the community struggle to welcome – or understand – what it is they are doing. But few people can really understand what motivates some of the most hardened athletes in the world to run around a single city block day after day.

And that is the beauty of the Self Transcendence 3100 Mile Race. Because, unlike every other race in this book, the overarching goal is not to go further or faster than anyone else (although there is an element to it of that), but rather to reach 'new levels of inner and outer perfection'. And so the athletes run the same course. That course is a mere 883m (0.5488 miles, about 2900 feet) long, and to finish the race athletes will have to complete 5649 laps. Most will notch up at least 1600km (1000 miles), some will make it all the way through to the end. But that end is exactly where they started from, and that is the point of the race.

The mental pressure that this places on the competitors is immense. Most ultra-distance runners are able to lose themselves in the ever-changing scenery; scenery that offers a brief respite when things get really tough. Competitors in the Self Transcendence 3100 have no such refuge. A highway thunders past part of the course; school children routinely mock the runners' efforts; violent crime in the neighbourhood is not unknown; and at all times they have to move in, out and around any of the pedestrians or cyclists that take to pavements of this block.

What's more, the time pressure placed on runners is immense. To successfully complete the race, an athlete must cover a minimum of 97km (60 miles) per day. That is a huge amount of mileage to be tackling day after day, and one that will eventually force many of the small field of starters out of the event.

right Competitors change direction each day to avoid injury

above 60 miles a day every day. Only the strongest – of body and mind – can overcome the challenge

Needless, to say, for those who overcome the mental pressures, the physical strain of completing a race of this distance is enormous. The 3100 is run exclusively along the concrete sidewalks of Jamaica. One of the hardest surfaces to run on, concrete is purportedly 10 times harder than asphalt (the usual surfaces of roads). This places a massive physical strain on the body, with legs having to deal with day after day of repetitive pounding.

What's more this is real street running. Competitors have to negotiate the street like any other pedestrian (or casual athlete). As such, they have to be mindful of the litter that lines the pavements; any obstacles that may miraculously appear during the 52 days (car crashes are not uncommon); and the fumes of the cars that run along the highway. Under this sort of physical strain, the last thing that a runner needs is to have to quickly change direction or speed because of a previously unknown hindrance on the course.

Of course, there is little that the organisers can do to mitigate the effects of concrete on the limbs or litter on the pavements, but they do alternate the direction of the race each day to ensure that athletes do not pick up any repetitive strain injuries as a result of running and turning the same way over and over again. Other than that – and the aid stations that line the route – the rest comes down to each athlete's mind and body.

The Self Transcendence 3100 mile really is a race that lives up to its name. And the achievements of the few competitors who have completed the course speak volumes of the mental and physical prowess of those involved. Since the race was increased from 2700 miles (4345km) to 3100 miles (4989km) in 1996, Madhupran Wolfgang Schwek has owned the world record, breaking his 2002 best (42 days, 13 hours, 23 minutes and 3 seconds) with a time of 41 days,

8 hours 16 minutes and 29 seconds in 2006. Suprbha Beckjord holds the women's record with 49 days, 14 hours, 30 minutes and 54 seconds. She is also the only person to have completed every edition of the race.

An immense physical journey and an intense psychological challenge, the Self Transcendence 3100 pits athletes against one of the most mundane courses on the planet. To complete it, the athlete not only has to overcome intense physical pressure, but has to rise above all of the man-made obstacles placed in his or her way. Only then, can they claim to have truly understood the goal of the Self Transcendence 3100.

Stutisheel Lebedev

ATHLETE PERSPECTIVE

I first applied for the 3100-mile event in 2003, but didn't make it in. The following March I had a call to see if I wanted to participate in the 2004 race – which, with the race in June, didn't give me much time to prepare. But I felt it was my destiny to run and said yes! I undertook some race research, to see exactly what I needed to prepare. Completing the race in 2004 set me up to finish it a further eight times.

Before that 2004 race, the longest race I had completed was a 105km (65-mile) race in Moscow. You couldn't qualify for the 3100 today with that limited background; you would need to show potential in a six- to ten-day race first.

My training is year round and I run 5–11km (3–7 miles) every day, increasing the volume and quality from the beginning of March in preparation for the race. I run up to 160km (100 miles) a week, also doing a range of knee- and back-strengthening exercises that help cope with the long distance.

In May I follow a detox/cleansing diet to clean the digestive system, which I find really helps the organs when under stress in the race. For the first 23 days, it's OK if the organs aren't cleansed, but in the second half of the race the extreme stress means cleansing can help.

For the 3100 you need to focus on a steady pace and get used to running at this slow pace. I initially found it hard and tiring to restrict my pace to this slow speed and have had to practise running like that. Now I have more experience, I am trying to increase my

average speed over the distance and so have added in a quality training session once a week, running 5km (3 miles) at top speed. Volume should always be the first consideration, though.

Mental preparation is key to the race; fundamentally, if you do something for such a long time, you need to love it. I've loved running since infancy, training in the beautiful woods in Ukraine, and I love being by nature. Peace of mind is important in the race; I've practised meditation for 20 years, which helps calm the mind. You can't go into the 3100 thinking you'll win or trying to compete with others. You need to establish your own schedule and maintain your peace of mind, competing with yourself to achieve self-transcendence.

Maintaining this state allows you to deal with any problems, and means the run becomes a joyous occasion. As I run, I feel access to the soul and inner contentment; doubts and insincerities fall away, and I'm really happy.

The 3100 is a unique race environment with all competitors pulling for each other. When I finish, it's a surprise and I'm not really excited, more like 'That's it'. While I run, I meditate better, require less sleep and generally just feel better. It's a tough race, but after a few months all you recall are the heavenly and positive experiences.

Stutisheel Lebedev is a multiple finisher of the Self Transcendence 3100 mile Race. For more information, visit 3100.lebedev.org.ua

SOUTH AMERICA

Type Multi-discipline
Date February
Distance 600km (372 miles)
Main obstacles Weather, technical, terrain
Website www.patagonianexpeditionrace.com
They call it The Last Wild Race

Competitors say
❝The PER epitomises what expedition adventure racing is: long unsupported outings in true wilderness.❞

Patagonian Expedition Race

A harsh environment, dramatic and ever-changing weather systems and one of the least inhabited regions on the planet: the Patagonian Expedition Race is a journey through – and challenge against – one of the few remaining wildernesses.

below One in all in

opposite Patagonia offers a stunning backdrop

Patagonia is a true wilderness. Straddling Chile and Argentina, it is a land that few people ever get to see, and one where even fewer live. The weather is unpredictable and the terrain inhospitable. But it is spectacular, providing the stage for one of the toughest adventure races in the world.

Launched in 2004, the Patagonian Expedition Race pits 20 teams of four individuals against this remarkable region – and each other. Along the route, teams tackle multiple disciplines as they cover more than 600km (372 miles) of terrain. The race takes place in the middle of the Southern Hemisphere's summer (Patagonia is just 1500km/932 miles from Antarctica), when the daylight can extend for up to 17 hours, making physical and mental demands of the event relentless.

What's more, the team nature of the competition places added physical and mental strain on those who take part. Each team must be comprised of four individuals. Every team must start and finish the race together, and if any of the competitors are unable to finish one of the stages, then the whole team is forced to pull out. Not only does this place a huge amount of emphasis on the importance of teamwork (particularly in a physically demanding environment), it also places pressure on the individual team members. In a region that is difficult to prepare for, failure is not an option unless a competitor is willing to jeopardise the success of his or her teammates.

Competition against other teams aside, the main challenge in the Patagonian Expedition Race is surviving the environment. River valleys, towering rocks, glaciers and fjords need to be tackled by the teams as they find themselves in places most people have only ever read about or seen on TV: the Southern Continental Ice Field, the Strait of Magellan, Torres del Paine, Tierra del Fuego, the Beagle Channel and Cape Horn; these are all places that inspire and astonish.

The reality, though, can be more down to earth, as the variable weather conditions often soak and freeze athletes through the days of competition.

Dealing with – and overcoming – this environment requires a significant level of technical ability. The route is kept secret up until the night before the race starts meaning that first-class navigational skills are required. GPS is forbidden during the race, and so competitors have to use a good old-fashioned map and compass. Using these basic tools to plot the fastest route through the hugely varying

terrain can be more important than pure physical fitness. The fastest aren't always those who can move quickest, but often those who take the shortest route.

And it's not just navigating while on a steady walk; disciplines in the race vary dramatically. Of course, trekking is a mandatory part of the event, and all teams will spend a large amount of their time on foot. But as well as trekking there are elements of technical mountain biking, rope work and kayaking, all of which competitors must be able to manage by themselves.

As such, kayakers must be able to demonstrate proficiency in the waters, and the ability to recover themselves should they capsize in what are dangerous seas. Likewise, anyone involved in the race has to be certified in ascent, rappelling, Tyrolese and fixed ropes. While some adventure races incorporate rope work as something of a gimmick, the Patagonian Expedition does nothing of the sort. Where athletes are forced to engage with the ropes, they do so for a very good reason.

The terrain and environment of Patagonia is wild. But that doesn't mean that the organisers are an ever-present entity on the course. Far from it. For massive stretches of the race, teams are, for all intents and purposes, alone. Of

above The changeable weather is a constant concern

course, they may come across the competition as they move through the course, but teams have to be self-sufficient between checkpoints. That is why the list of equipment which every team (and competitor) has to carry is so extensive. This equipment ranges from a satellite phone to a four-man tent, first-aid items to the prerequisite clothes needed to deal with the changing weather and climate. And that is before nutrition and hydration is factored into the equation. All of this has to be divided up between the team members and carried with them at all times, adding yet another variable to an already difficult race.

But while teams are guaranteed spectacular surrounds, one thing they cannot be certain of is the course. The route, and so each of the distances, for the Patagonian Expedition changes from year to year, making historical comparisons between the teams and their achievements difficult. What is guaranteed, though, is that the race attracts some of the fastest, toughest teams of adventure racers on the planet.

A spectacular test of human endurance, the Patagonian Expedition Race pits mankind against some of the most stunning terrain on the planet. With variable – and extreme – weather to match, competitors have to work together across a variety of disciplines to overcome a beautiful and demanding challenge. But those who succeed know that they have squared up to one of the most spectacular regions on earth, and they have lived to tell the tale.

Mark Lattanzi

I think that adventure racers 'train' in a fundamentally different way from other endurance athletes like runners or triathletes. I am no exception. I don't have a set training plan for getting ready for a race. It's more that my entire life is built around the activities of adventure racing, and I tend to do some form of activity every day.

Preparing for the Patagonian Expedition Race is always a challenge. It's a hard race – bordering on a survival event as much as a race. So, the question of what to carry becomes more serious. For shorter, easier races, lighter is almost always better. For PER, the conditions can get so extreme that I tend to err on the side of safer rather than lighter. Having a dry fleece to put on can be the difference between continuing and dropping out of the race.

It's a challenge to go back – to know that you'll be trekking for days and everything you have is going to get wet and probably stay wet. Visiting Patagonia was a childhood dream of mine. I remember reading about it in school. It sounded like another planet to me: big colourful plants spread out across river valleys, towering monoliths of rock, glaciers and fjords. And all at the end of the Earth. I dreamed of going there and exploring it. Thirty years later, in 2009, I finally made it there. And it was as amazing as I'd hoped. Many times during the 2009 PER, I felt like we were in places no human had ever been before (except, of course, for the three teams in front of us). It was beautiful. It was challenging. I loved it.

In the 2011 PER, we faced all the challenges that the race director planned for us – lake side traverses, steep canyons to descend, rivers to cross and many more. We also had the issue of one of my teammates losing her thyroid medication on the first day of the race. As the race went on, she had a harder time of maintaining enough energy to continue and to regulate her body temperature. As a team, we did all we could – taking her pack and towing, but it was clear that we needed to pull out of the race.

Competing in the PER has been one of the highlights of my adventure racing career. I have done the race twice. During the race, we've traversed vast river valleys full of crazy colourful vegetation (the turba), hiked around glacial lakes full of floating ice, seen elephant seals, penguins, foxes and the iconic huemul. We kayaked with whales in the Strait of Magellan, camped on a glacier in a mountain pass, and rappelled off a cliff into frigid ocean waters. During one leg in 2009, after running out of food, we even foraged for berries for a few hours so we could continue going.

The PER epitomises what expedition adventure racing is: long unsupported outings in true wilderness.

Mark Lattanzi is an adventure racer who came fourth in the 2009 Patagonian Expedition Race. For more information, visit www.marklattanzi.com.

Type Foot
Date October
Distance 220km (137 miles)
Main obstacles Terrain, Heat
Website www.junglemarathon.com
They call it Discover a spectacular part of this vast country and see first-hand the wonders of nature.

Competitors say
'Completely crazy, completely chaotic, and if you're into this type of race you have to do it.'

Jungle Marathon

Poisonous trees, territorial jaguars, swamps, mountains and a breathless heat push competitors to the edge of human endurance in a bid to conquer one of the most unforgiving environments on Earth.

below The ascents and descents are brutally challenging

The Amazon Jungle is one of the most inhospitable places on the planet. Stretching across nine countries and home to one in ten of the world's plant and animal species, the Amazon is a place few humans have the opportunity to explore.

Participants in the Jungle Marathon do. A self-supported multi-day race that takes in six stages over seven days (the longest stage is 89km/55 miles), the Jungle Marathon weaves a path through the mighty Amazon, with camps being set in either remote clearings or local villages. The course might change from year to year, but one fact remains: competitors are truly immersed. Not only in the culture, but also in the life and death of the world's most famous rainforest.

The Amazon contains some of the most spectacular, deadly and awe-inspiring plants and animals on earth. Spiders, snakes, fire ants and mosquitoes are par for the course (and camps) en route. Jaguars, crocodiles and piranhas may be less abundant, but certainly lurk in the trees, rivers and swamps that competitors are forced to tackle. Needless to say, the flora isn't much better. Spiky – and sometimes poisonous – trees and plants are commonplace, with medics routinely required to extract thorns up to 3cm (1.2 inches) long from feet, legs and arms.

And there is no way to avoid some of these obstacles. There are no manicured paths in the Jungle Marathon. The route is, of course, marked by ribbons. But participants are frequently required to climb over, under or round fallen trees as the course twists through the jungle. That course is incredibly hilly, with competitors often required to ascend and descend perilously steep slopes. With precarious, uneven footing (not to mention unfriendly fauna), descending these slopes is often tougher than climbing them. What's more, when they do make it to the foot of a slope, there is usually a river or a swamp waiting for them.

As such, being 'wet' is par for the course, and competitors must be able to cope with running in a constantly sodden state. In some respects this

above Crossing
rivers at least helps
competitors cool off

right What lies
beneath ...

helps to mitigate the sternest challenge the Jungle Marathon offers (heat), but also places strain on the body and the feet in particular. Blisters are a common – and potentially race-threatening – complaint with the constant damp taking its toll on hot, sweaty skin.

But it is the heat that is undoubtedly the most challenging – and dangerous – variable in the Jungle Marathon. Temperatures regularly exceed 40°C (104°F) and in this damp, windless environment heat exhaustion and dehydration can easily end the race of even the fittest competitors. As such, IV drips are commonplace at the conclusion of a stage – although, predictably for a race this tough, the use of an IV drip incurs a two-hour penalty. Of course, in the presence of such dangers the organisers enlist an extensive team of medical staff, who are trained to tackle everything from a rotting heel to complete physical collapse.

Between the start and finish points of the stages, competitors are expected to be entirely self-sufficient. And to protect themselves against some of the challenges faced during the race, they are required to carry an extensive list of equipment on every stage. Ranging from food and water to first-aid equipment and basic survival gear, this merely adds a further burden to the participants, with rucksacks weighing anything up to 10kg (22lb). Any items that are listed as mandatory but not carried by a competitor incur a penalty, and because of the dangers posed by the jungle, organisers are keen to ensure all athletes play by their rules.

Race stages vary in distance from 16km to 89km (10–55 miles), but the shortest are not necessarily the easiest – or the fastest. And while the route is marked, all competitors are expected to be able to navigate themselves safely through the jungle. As with many self-supported ultra-distance races,

below An unforgiving environment awaits competitors

below Anything goes when it comes to establishing the route

stage some athletes have been known to have retired from the race due to hypothermia. On the other side, the lightning-fast descent of Irazu pushes both the mechanical and mental strength of the athletes and bikes to their thresholds. Once the third stage is complete, the riders are nearly home. Stage Four is a relative breeze, with the second half of the stage being a flat run in to the Caribbean. However, with the best part of 386km (240 miles) of riding and 11,887m (39,000 feet) of climbing in their legs, 'relative breeze' is a relative term.

This is, of course, the ideal route. Because of the sheer breadth of ecosystems that the course passes through, it is not uncommon for organisers to have to change the course due to natural – and sometimes man-made – problems.

And that is, in essence, why the race began in the first place. Like so many of the challenges in this book, this race is founded on one person's desire to make a change. In this instance it was Roman Urbina, who wanted to highlight the plight of Costa Rica's endangered wildlife. Competitors on the course not only face an epic physical challenge, they are also confronted with some of the most spectacular sites in nature. Travelling through nine microclimates that house five per cent of the Earth's birds, plants and animals (in 0.01 per cent of the Earth's landmass), La Ruta de los Conquistadores provides an ecological insight into the biodiversity of one of the world's most spectacular countries. As long as your legs aren't burning too much and you can still see clearly.

La Ruta de los Conquistadores is truly an epic challenge that embraces the essence of adventure. Leg-sapping climbs through diverse microclimates, hair-raising descents down the sides of volcanoes, tracks that demand your bike is carried (not ridden), and the ever-looming threat of a cut-off time. There's a reason why this race is so legendary, and that reason is because it is indisputably tough.

right One of the toughest mountain bike races on earth

Todd Wells

What a race! La Ruta was everything it was billed as and more. The climbs go on forever! And they are super steep! Like 'How am I going to ride up that?' steep. And just finding the correct way on the course is a challenge, the direction signs are small, and if you're not with a motorbike or someone that knows the course, good luck. The hiking wasn't bad, just a lot of on and off the bike. The railroad bridges were crazy, not because you're going to fall off, but it's very easy to slip and cut your leg or foot on the old ties.

Oh yeah, you might get your bike stolen at gunpoint as well or get stung by a bunch of bees while crossing one of the bridges. All that said, it was awesome.

I was lucky to have a great first day and get enough time to hang onto the jersey for the rest of the week. On Day Two, I was still pretty good but had some bad luck with a flat tyre and lost time to the guy in second. Day Three, we climbed for what seemed like forever and I was in the box the whole way. One competitor had me under pressure for all 2100m (7000 feet) of the volcano climb. Luckily I caught him on the descent and he cracked less then 10km (6 miles) from the finish, so I gained half the time back I had lost to him the day before. The last day had two climbs at the start (about 15–20 minutes each) that hurt really bad. I came off a bit on the second steep dirt road climb but was able to get back on before the flat section of road, dirt road, railroad tracks and beach.

Then there was my support crew, they were the key to everything. We had two land cruisers fully decked out with Thule racks and boxes. I had both my Stumpjumper 29, which I raced the first two days, and my Epic 29, which I raced the last two days.

The crew would make it to each aid station regardless of how remote or how fast they would have to drive to get there. They almost flipped the vehicle multiple times on the steep, muddy dirt roads used to access a lot of the zones. There are no street signs or addresses in most of the places we went in Costa Rica and the course map is almost non-existent, so if you don't have local knowledge, you're not going anywhere.

After racing around all day to feed me and give technical assistance, they would completely rebuild my bike to get it ready for the next day. Meg would clean all my other stuff and the Specialized crew would do store runs and whatever else was needed, including taking care of their normal jobs. And did I mention the races started at 6 a.m., so we would normally be up by 4.30 a.m.? The team was incredible.

The Costa Rican people were awesome, and it was cool to catch the race on the news at night while flipping through the channels. The scenery was great and finishing at the Caribbean sea on the last day in Limon was definitely a highlight. We rode on the beach for eight of the last 10km (five of the last six miles) and it was awesome.

Todd Wells won the 2011 La Ruta de Conquistadores in 17 hours, 18 minutes and 6 seconds. Todd has competed at two Olympics and won numerous UCI events.

ARCTICA

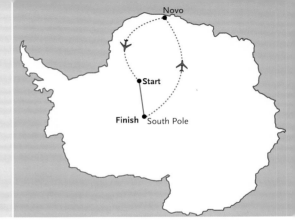

Type Ski and Foot
Date January to February
Distance 777.8 km (420 nautical miles)
Main obstacles Weather, altitude, cold
Website www.extremeworldraces.com
They Call It The Ultimate Extreme Endurance Race

Competitors say
You're on your own in one of the most inhospitable places on the planet. It's not like you can just pop home for a cup of tea or anything like that.

The Extreme World Races South Pole Race

Temperatures of −40°C (−40°F), hurricane-force winds, blinding snowstorms and a trek across the infamous Polar Plateau make the EWR South Pole Race a true test of human endurance.

below Just like the original 'race', the competition is fierce

The bravest men of the 19th and early 20th centuries had two things on their mind: exploration and fortune. While many went west, a very small number gazed south: Antarctica. Numerous explorers were driven back – or killed – by this dangerous, desolate and largely uncharted continent. But the quest for geographical and scientific discovery – as well as the desire to place a flag on the Pole – was sufficient motivation.

So it was that in 1911 Roald Amundsen and Robert Falcon Scott began their now infamous race to the South Pole. They were two of the most celebrated explorers of their time, and what happened during that fateful race has been comprehensively documented. Amundsen arrived at the Pole some 35 days ahead of the Briton and returned to Norway a hero. Scott's team all perished on the return leg, his name now synonymous with the death of British exploration.

It is against this backdrop that the EWR South Pole Race is run. Admittedly, the route differs substantially from the

original expedition run by both Scott and Amundsen, but the objectives remain largely the same. Teams battle it out across one of the most inhospitable environments on the planet to reach their ultimate goal: the Pole.

As with all of the toughest challenges in the world, completing the journey is just one part of the South Pole Race. To have put in the months of mental and physical preparation that enable you to stand on the Geographical South Pole is the achievement (regardless of where you place in the race).

The training and preparations that go into the South Pole Race are extreme. Up to 17 teams of three people are eligible to enter the race. Each team member is required to take part in a mandatory Polar training programme in Norway. During this week – in conditions as similar to Antarctica as is possible in Europe – competitors receive instruction on cross-country skiing, kit preparation and cold weather management. In addition, the teams learn how to manage and handle their pulk (or sledge) – an essential piece of Polar kit, but one that must be controlled with utmost skill.

Away from Norway, athletes engage in months of physical training – preparing their bodies to drag hundreds of kilograms of kit across the tough, high-altitude terrain.

And the preparations continue in the south. Following the trip to the Russian scientific outpost of NOVO (from Cape Town, competitors take a freight plane), it is time to acclimatise to Antarctica. If the conditions and the environment are not daunting enough, the very real danger facing competitors up on the Antarctic plateau is.

Then it begins.

above A stunningly desolate landscape awaits

With a start line nearly 3000m (9800 feet) above sea
level, altitude is yet another factor to throw into the mix.
The first leg of the race is approximately 345km (215 nautical
miles). As soon as competitors cross the start line, they are,
for all intents and purposes, on their own.

Antarctica is a unique and challenging environment. It
is one of the few places on the planet where katabatic winds
of 130km/h (80mph) can hurtle down the Polar Plateau,
snowstorms can lead to a complete whiteout in a matter of
seconds and temperatures can plummet as low as −40°C
(−40°F). Along the route, snow bridges form precarious
paths across deep, dark crevasses. Tales of frostbite,
pneumonia and snow blindness suddenly become a reality,
and all the while the teams are forced to push on regardless
– conscious that they have a limited amount of supplies and

a very long, arduous journey ahead of them before they
reach the midway break. This places an immense physical
and psychological strain on competitors.

Some 345km (215 miles) into the race, the teams are
forced to stop for 24 hours at the halfway point, resting and
resupplying ahead of the push for the Pole – another 345km
(215 miles) away.

From here, it starts to get really tough. The altitude
increases – as does the cold – and the snow gets deeper
way up on the plateau. Then there is the landscape.
Miles and miles of blinding terrain, stretching off into
the distance beneath a temperamental sky. Add to that
fatigue, niggles and injuries sustained during the opening
march, and you have a recipe for a truly tough, thoroughly
daunting challenge. But one that most involved in the race

will conquer. As the teams near their goal, the scientific bases that surround the area start to spring up. And there, in the midst of it all, is the simple sign that displays the achievements (and thoughts) of the two men who led the first successful expeditions to the Geographical South Pole: Roald Amundsen and Robert Falcon Scott.

The EWR South Pole Race harks back to the mystery and majesty of the early 20th-century explorers. Of course, the technology these days is somewhat different and the route is slightly shorter. But for 35 days (if you are quick), competitors face up to the raw reality of an epic march through one of the most inhospitable environments on the planet. They conquer mental, physical and environmental challenges that many people would struggle to simply comprehend. And they do it in the name of competition – and achievement.

Matt Elliott

To prepare for the Race to the South Pole, I took the advice of some personal trainers and I've been trying to build up a bit of body mass. When you're down there, you're going to lose 13–19kg (2–3 stone) during the race. I wanted to put on muscle mass rather than too much fat, so at first it was a case of working out in the gym five or six days a week. Then in the last four months I've been pulling a tyre around the local park trying to simulate the strains on my back of pulling a sledge.

For cold weather preparation we went out to Switzerland, but unfortunately they were in the middle of a heat wave. We found a glacier that was about 10–15°C (50–60°F) at the top of it, which meant we didn't really get a chance to try our kit out in the cold. We also spent one week training up in Norway, where we learnt a lot of the technical aspects of preparation.

But after that it is almost up to the individual to work out how to mentally and physically prepare yourself.

The mental preparation is probably tougher, as it is the big unknown. To be honest, it's also one of the reasons for signing up this event: to see how far I could push myself mentally. Training for that has involved thinking just about the race every day for almost the last 18 months. You start thinking about what it's like and what it's going to be like. For me, –40°C (–40°F), that's just a number. I have no idea of understanding how cold –40°C (–40°F) is because I've never been in temperatures like that, dragging a sledge for 12–14 hours per day. This is one of the things that drew me to the race: the mental challenge when you're low and on a down, that you have to keep pushing because there is no way out. You're on your own in one of the most inhospitable places on the planet. It's not like you can just pop home for a cup of tea or anything like that. You just have to push on.

The unknown is definitely one of the fears, though. I'm quite organised and I do like structure and I'm going into an environment that I know very little about. I don't know how I'm going to handle it. I know how I want to handle it, and I have obviously got the image of going down there, strolling along for 12 hours a day and making it look easy. But in reality I'm more worried that I'm going to get out there and the cold is going to be bone chilling and the days are going to be endless. And I'm worried about whether I can do it. The race is long, it is in a hostile place and there's not much support. It is the complete unknown.

Matt Elliott competed in the EWR South Pole Race in January 2012.

CROSS-
NTINENT

Type Rowing
Date December
Distance 4100km (2549 miles)
Main obstacles Distance, weather, mental, currents
Website www.woodvale-challenge.com
They call it A once-in-a-lifetime challenge that pushes competitors beyond their mental and physical limits.

Competitors say
There's certainly no feeling like waking up for the first time and not being able to see land in any direction.

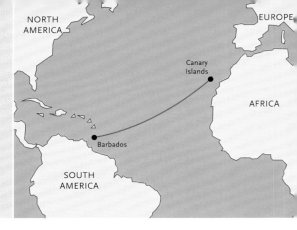

Woodvale Challenge

A minimum of 4100km (2549 miles) across some of the most ferocious waters in the world, nothing and nobody for miles around, and only you and your partner moving you forwards. The Woodvale Challenge is a true test of human physical and psychological endurance.

For centuries, the Atlantic Ocean has challenged the bravery and skill of the navigators who attempt to cross her. Of course, most are allowed to pass. But every now and again, the ocean claims the lives of a small number, and in so doing reminds us of her awesome power and potential.

It is this power and potential that faces competitors of the Woodvale Challenge. A truly relentless event that sees solo participants and pairs attempt to cross the Atlantic from the Canary Islands to Antigua – otherwise known as the Columbus route. As the bird flies, this route is 4100km (2549 miles) from point to point. But as the rowing boat bobs – and is subjected to the currents and storms that often plague the mid-Atlantic – most competitors can expect to cover in excess of 4800km (3000 miles) in over 70 days.

The challenge is formidable on every level.

Physically, competitors spend weeks, months and sometimes years building themselves up to take on some of the toughest conditions on earth. And for the most part, the physicality and conditions the rowers are going to face are completely unknown. The only things that the rowers can do in preparation are to bulk themselves up (giving their bodies plenty of mass to feed on) and train at long-distance events. But while rowers are famous for their relentless training regimens, the simple fact is that few will tackle a training session that is even one-hundredth of the distance of the Woodvale in one go.

What's more, when they are out on the ocean the routine is both relentless and painful. Competitors tend to sleep and row in two-hour shifts. This places a massive physical and psychological strain on the individual. The constant spray of the ocean salt causes sores that burn through the skin following hour upon hour of metronomic action. These impressive welts are similar to the blisters contracted by runners, and their debilitating impact can be massive on an athlete dealing with fatigue in the face of unforgiving elements.

And it is the elements that truly govern the progress of competitors in the race. The event is scheduled to take place at the most favourable time of the year. But storms of varying strength are common, and it is not impossible for boats to face up to 9m (30-foot) waves. These storms can also lead to extremes of temperature, which places a further strain on fatigued bodies.

But it is the mental side of the race that is, perhaps, the most challenging. No amount of physical preparation can prepare competitors for the sight of thousands of miles of completely empty ocean. Of course, on occasion there is a passing ship. But if it comes close it generally has to be dodged as opposed to welcomed. The Columbus Route is one of the quickest across the Atlantic, and so is one of the busiest. All competitors have to be conscious of the threat posed by these massive ships, and be constantly vigilant when out on the open ocean.

Like many ultra-distance events, the preparation of the equipment is key in the Woodvale. From the outset competitors have to ensure that they have everything they

below Nothing but sea and sky for miles around

opposite The demands are relentless

need for a completely unassisted crossing of the Atlantic. The organisers of the Woodvale Challenge provide weather updates – and that's it. Once a boat leaves the Canaries, the crew is, for all intents and purposes, alone. So, should anything go wrong with the boat, with supplies or even with a crew member, they have to be prepared to manage their own well-being until help can arrive (which may take hours – or even days).

The fastest boats will cross the Atlantic in little more than 70 days, the slowest can take much longer. All will face tremendous challenges along the way, which will push them to the very edge of their physical and mental abilities. And all will have an epic story to tell at the end of the Woodvale Challenge – a truly formidable feat of human endurance.

left The sunset is always there to be enjoyed

Ben Thackwray

Psychologically, nothing will prepare you! You need to be well rehearsed with every system on the boat and what to do in every situation, so if something goes wrong you don't have that natural blind panic. But to be honest, even if you are well prepared in this sense, there's certainly no feeling like waking up for the first time and not being able to see land in any direction!

The biggest obstacles are getting the boat ready. You never feel like you've done everything and you can agonise forever, thinking, 'Would that be better here, or here?' or 'What if we had a ...?' Although this is perfectly natural, experience now tells me that this is just anxiety rather than things not being ready.

Actually, after a while everything becomes routine. You get used to big waves smashing over the boat, you trust the boat, you get used to sleeping and rowing in two-hour shifts, you get comfortable with your surroundings and you get to watch the sunrise and sunset every day – and the most amazing crystal clear skies at night, which is fantastic!

But it isn't easy. When I first rowed the Atlantic in 2007/8, we had a number of problems. Both our water makers stopped working and we had to hand-pump water through a desalinator, which is extremely inefficient. We had an electrical storm one night, which meant that we were sitting in a carbon-fibre boat surrounded by nothing else for miles and miles – we just had to turn everything off and keep our fingers crossed! We also had our rudder smashed off, not once but twice by something huge underneath the boat! After the first time we managed to fix it with the correct spare parts, but the second time we had no spares, so we had to improvise a fix with something that was meant for a different part of the boat.

All of these obstacles are part and parcel of the challenge. Finishing the row – bedraggled and exhausted – rowing into the historic English Harbour in Antigua surrounded by mega-yachts was incredible. It was bittersweet, though, because I was enjoying the experience so much I didn't want it to end.

So much so that I've been working towards getting back in a rowing boat ever since.

Ben Thackwray rowed the Atlantic in 2007 as part of an 'Adventure Trilogy'. He summited Mount Everest in 2011 and intends to ski to the South Pole. Find out more about Ben at benthackwray.com.

Type Foot | **Date** Varies
Distance 250km (155 miles)
Main obstacles Hot, cold, terrain, distance, weather, mental
Website www.4deserts.com
What it takes Competitors are challenged to go beyond the limits of their physical and mental endurance.

Competitors say
All of the races have got their different challenges.

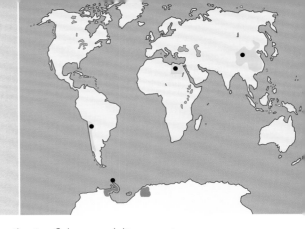

4 Deserts

Four deserts, four races. All last seven days and take place over 250km (155 miles) of the world's most demanding terrain. From extreme highs in temperature to life-threatening lows, the 4 Deserts is a true test of human endurance and physical adaptability.

below Antarctica offers unique mental and physical challenges

For most people, the thought of running 250km (155 miles) over seven days across a desert is extreme. For a select few, the goal is to conquer at least two such marathons with a view of qualifying for a unique race: a 250km (155-mile) ultra- marathon in the coldest desert on earth. That is the premise of the 4 Deserts series. Athletes must complete at least two from the Atacama Crossing in Chile, the Gobi March in China and the Sahara Race in Egypt in a bid to qualify for The Last Desert (Antarctica): a gruelling race on the icy continent.

While the demands of racing the 4 Deserts series are obvious, the rules on completing them are not. Athletes, for instance, do not have to complete the deserts in any

particular order (Antarctica not included). Instead, they are
free to race Atacama, Gobi and the Sahara as they wish and
over a protracted period of time. Of course, some choose
to tackle all three qualifying events – plus the Last Desert
(Antarctica) – in one year, and so claim the 4 Deserts Grand
Slam. But attempting the Grand Slam places immense
physical pressure on the body, and both recovery and
preparation for the next race is essential.

Each desert carries its own individual challenges, making
the physical and mental barriers to completion huge. The

body is expected not only to push on through a multi-stage
ultra-distance event, but to do so across demanding terrain
and in extremes of heat and cold. The mental strain that
desert racing places on the shoulders of the athletes is
immense, with individuals having to focus on their physical
well-being as much as the challenges of what can be miles
of featureless horizon.

And few areas of the world can place as much mental
and physical strain on an individual as the Sahara Desert. It
is the hottest race of the series, with temperatures frequently

exceeding 50°C (122°F) on a course that is largely run over sand and dunes. Over the seven days, the 160 or so competitors race stages of varying distance – the longest 80km (50-miles) in length – finishing the week in the shadows of the Pyramids of Giza.

The desert may not be as hot, but the demands that the Gobi places on athletes are just as extreme. The oldest race of the series, competitors are presented with terrain that ranges from dusty tracks to rock-strewn riverbeds, with some river crossings thrown in for good measure. Like the Sahara, the Gobi experiences extremes of temperatures and in the desolate landscape there are few places to shelter from the 45°C (113°F) heat.

From heat to height: the Atacama Desert is the driest on the planet, and can also get pretty hot at 40°C (104°F); it is also the highest in the series. It offers a course that 'enjoys' sharp ascents and descents, competitors rarely venturing below 2300m (7545 feet) above sea level – adding into the mix the demands of running at altitude.

Once these three races are completed, all that remains is The Last Desert; an entirely different beast altogether. Run biannually, the race takes place on a course that varies depending on the weather conditions. And those conditions can be extreme. Temperatures can easily fall as low as –20°C (–4°F), and fierce Antarctic winds can make racing impossible. Most of the actual event takes place on snow,

and stages can vary from 1.5km (0.9-mile) loops, which present a unique challenge, to longer, testing circuits. Unlike the other races, The Last Desert is not a point-to-point due to the conditions of Antarctica. The race schedule is also flexible because of the weather, athletes having to be prepared to race at very short notice, and to be pulled from the course as soon as the weather begins to turn.

Four deserts, four challenges. To complete one is impressive, to complete all four remarkable. Not only is the sheer ability to run 250km (155 miles) a thorough examination of an individual's credentials, but to manage nutrition and hydration in extreme conditions is a challenge in itself. Add to that the unique terrain that is nigh-on impossible to prepare for, and the importance of mental conditioning becomes clear.

What's more, this is very much a race. While many competitors choose to run/walk certain stages, a number of the world's top ultra runners compete for what is a prestigious title. Even for those who aren't going for the win, the 4 Deserts Grand Slam is a very special achievement in its own right.

A true test of human endurance, adaptability and mental fortitude, the 4 Deserts is rightly renowned as one of the toughest race series on the planet. Those who complete it can truly say that they have suffered, survived and conquered a challenge which is beyond the majority of people in the world.

Ryan Sandes

I think every race you do, you have to try and look at the specific challenges of that race. Are you running with altitude? Are you running with 50°C (122°F) heat or in sub-zero temperatures? All of the races have got their different challenges.

A large part of these races are mental – at least 40–45 per cent. So you have to go into a race like that being as positive as possible. You have to realise it's going to be tough and is a challenge, and if you go into it and think 'I'm not going to enjoy it', then you aren't going to enjoy it. But if you go into it thinking that it's a challenge and something to try and overcome, then you are going to have your highs and lows but really just make the most of them and enjoy being part of an awesome environment.

I think physically the Gobi was the toughest desert for me because my body wasn't used to doing a multi-day, self-supporting race and it was the first race that I did in the 4 Deserts series. From that point of view, it was really tough. But also the conditions were really tough. It was really hot in the Gobi and also the terrain is quite varied – it was quite up and down and some of it quite rocky and some of it sandy. So you never quite knew what to expect. Also, getting used to a self-supporting race is quite difficult because running 250km (155 miles) is hard enough, but having to do it self-supported makes it even more challenging.

Physically the Gobi is one of the toughest, but mentally Antarctica was tougher: it was a completely different race. You live off a boat for the 10 days that you're out there. And there are so many different factors. For instance, some of the guys got seasick, so you've got that in the back of your mind. Nothing was too planned because of the weather. So you're off an island and the weather is bad, so you could be sitting around for 12 hours and then all of a sudden an announcement would come through a loudspeaker that said 'You're going to start Stage One in three hours' and you don't have time to prepare.

In most races, you run from point A to B, so you are running a distance. In Antarctica, you run in times. So instead of running A to B you're running a whole bunch of circuits for an amount of time. They do that because the weather changes so frequently. So some of those days you'd do 5–9-mile (8.5–15km) loops but some of them are 1-mile (1.5km) loops. Also, once or twice we got called off early from the stage, so you never know how to pace yourself. It is unconventional and you couldn't control anything. In a race like that, you want to have everything pre-planned, but you have to go with the flow. You have to deal with that.

Among his many ultra-distance achievements, Ryan Sandes is the first person to win all four deserts. The South African also holds the course record for the Atacama Crossing. For more information, visit ryansandes.com.

Type Sailing
Date November
Distance 72,000km (39,000 miles)
Main obstacles Weather, mental, cold, distance
Website www.volvooceanrace.com
They call it The Everest of sailing.

Competitors say
I'm not sure that there are many sporting events that last nine months, so just getting to the end of it is an achievement in its own right.

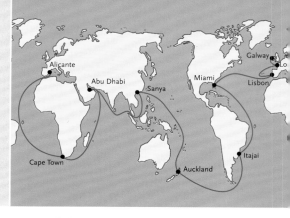

Volvo Ocean Race

Brutal seas, extremes of temperatures and no help for miles around. The crews of the Volvo Ocean Race tackle one of the ultimate endurance races on the planet, not to mention one of the most dangerous.

below Every crew member holds a crucial role

In the 1800s, fearless seamen used square riggers to transport their goods around the world. 'Racing' from port to port, they covered the greatest distance in the shortest time possible in a bid to maximise the profits from their lengthy trips. The exploits of these pioneering sailors – along with the later achievements of the likes of Sir Robin Knox Johnson and Sir Francis Chichester – inspired the sailing community.

Talk of a fully crewed race around the world quickly became reality when, in 1973, the Whitbread Round the World Race was launched.

Despite the loss of three crewmen in that first year, the organisers and competitors were not to be deterred, and the race soon became a regular fixture on the nautical calendar. Volvo came onboard for the 2001 race (renaming it the Volvo Ocean Race) and the race continues to capture the imaginations of both the sailing community and the world at large. Taking place every three years and over approximately nine months, the Volvo Ocean Race is a 72,000km (39,000-mile) 'sprint' around the world. Crews of 11 sailors tackle the nine-leg course that takes them from Alicante in Spain to Galway, Ireland via ports in Cape Town, Auckland and Miami (among others). En route, the ships will pass both the Cape of Good Hope and Cape Horn, as well as tackle the treacherous seas of the Southern Ocean.

But these landmarks tell only part of the story of what is a truly epic event. To have any chance of concluding a leg of the race – let alone an entire stage – crews and their skippers need to work in perfect unison against some of the most challenging ocean conditions.

The ocean can be brutal. The

conditions of the Atlantic and Pacific challenge many quite capable seamen at the best of times, with temperatures ranging from −5°C (23°F) to 40°C (104°F). However, those in the Southern Ocean are famously testing. From the Roaring Forties through to the Screaming Sixties (areas between the latitudes of 40 and 60° South), the wind and the waves can be ferocious. Air displaced from the equator heads south towards the Pole, picking up speed as it goes. What's more, there is little land to arrest the increasing speed of the wind in this part of the world, leading to some quite horrendous sailing conditions. Winds can easily reach 60 knots (110km/h, 70mph), and waves have been known to exceed 30m (100 feet) in height.

Compounding this, out in the Southern Ocean there is a distinct lack of help close at hand. In fact, that is the case on the majority of the nine legs. The crews have to be entirely self-sufficient, managing their own food, health and responses to emergencies for up to 20 days at a time. Of course, the competition is likely to be somewhere in the vicinity of a stricken boat (even if help – and a port – is not),

above The boats reach impressive speeds at sail

Type of event Multi-discipline
Date Varies
Distance of event 700–800km (435–500 miles)
Main obstacles Heat, cold, terrain, technical, weather
Website www.arworldseries.com
They call it The AR World Championship has defined the sport of adventure racing.

Competitors say
'It's a fantastic mental, physical and emotional journey.'

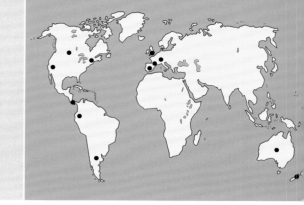

Adventure Racing World Series

From Argentina to Canada, England to Australia, the Adventure Racing World Series pushes the toughest endurance athletes to their limits on a journey into (almost) the complete unknown.

The Adventure Racing World Series (ARWS) is the pre-eminent adventure racing series on the planet. And there is a reason for that. For the most part it roams the globe, taking in different stops and culminating in a World Championship that is played out at a different location every year. What's more, most of the courses change year on year, their details released just 24 hours before the start to ensure no team gains an unfair advantage. And so to include one race in the Series we have to include them all. But, arguably, they all deserve a spot in a book about the toughest challenges on the planet.

The number of stops in the series varies year-on-year, but there are a few staple events in the United Kingdom, United States, Costa Rica, Switzerland and France. Other races, such as the Australian XPD, occur once every 18 months and so do not play a role in every series calendar. The top two teams in each event receive automatic qualification for the season-ending World Championships, and the rest of the field (of up to 70 teams) is made up of wildcards and private team entrants.

Despite the different locations and environments that the races are run over, a few core aspects of the races remain the same. Teams of four compete as a unit, never separated by more than 100m (330 feet) on any given stretch of the course. Once the gun goes off and the race begins, they are, for all intents and purposes, on their own. Every event in the ARWS is self-supported and teams have to pre-pack and plan everything needed for up to 10 days on the road. Of course, organisers arrange 'drops' where competitors can pick up the equipment and supplies they need to make it through to the next stage. But beyond that, what a team begins the race with, they must complete with. And the list of equipment that competitors have to include is enormous. Obviously, this is slightly dependent on the race itself (some are run up

near the Arctic Circle, others not too far from the equator), but the emphasis is on the fact that competitors have to be prepared, and be strong enough to carry additional weight on a demanding course.

And quite naturally, the courses are established to push them to the very limits. Every race involves elements of trekking, kayaking and mountain biking, and there are frequently additional pursuits added to spice things up. The courses are not marked, meaning it is the responsibility of each team to find their route to the various checkpoints across whatever terrain they come across. And the nature and type of terrain varies dramatically. From mountain passes to rainforest tracks, and from vast untouched forest land to sandy beaches, athletes in each race have to be able to tackle every obstacle that comes their way in whichever shape or form that materialises.

above The challenges are numerous and varied

opposite Tough challenges among spectacular scenery

below Each race has its own special challenges

Physically, the average adventure race pushes athletes way beyond the norm. The fastest teams – some of whom could be termed professionals – can complete the races in just over four days. During this period they will sleep for as little as seven hours (in total) and can burn in excess of 10,000 calories per day. The slower teams may take double that time but still only sleep for little more than four hours per day on average.

This lack of sleep, coupled with intense physical exertion, places a massive strain on the mind and body. Almost every competitor will encounter 'sleep monsters' en route to the finish line, and in extreme cases they may start to hallucinate. As such, every competitor will have to face up to their own individual demons. But they also have to work as a team. And this places pressure on every individual in the group. No matter how tired, injured or demotivated a competitor is, each of them must keep going for the sake of their team-mates.

As individual events, the various stages of the Adventure Racing World Series warrant mention in any book about the toughest challenges on the planet. As a combined series of events, the ARWS cements its place here. Pushing athletes to the very brink of human endurance, forcing them to work as a team at all stages, and casting them out into the complete unknown, the ARWS offers the perfect recipe for one of the ultimate physical challenges.

Nick Gracie

You can train for these races, but you can't replicate how hard it is because the hardness comes from racing like this for three or four days non-stop. You need to get your body used to sitting in the saddle or being on your feet or sitting in a kayak for a long time. And, obviously, the more of the races you do, the better you get at them and the more your body and brain get used to it.

I try to do specific training for races, but it can be difficult. Last year I did a race in Abu Dhabi in December. It was 45°C (113°F) in the desert and unbelievably hot, but I was training in November in the United Kingdom and it was really cold. So I went and did a lot of bikram yoga, which got my body used to hot conditions. When I went out training I would wear a lot of layers – so much that it was getting uncomfortable and I was getting really hot. I also trained a lot on sand tracks. I did a lot of running and riding a lot on them. It's hard to cycle on sand – especially soft sand – it's a real skill. It's still hard, though, because you're coming out of freezing conditions and going into heat.

Then, two months after Abu Dhabi, we were racing in Patagonia, which was brutally cold. It was OK because we had been back in England for a month, but even the United Kingdom in winter is not like going to Patagonia, which is unbelievably windy. My training for that – bizarrely as I am pretty fit – was to put on weight.

In all these races, though, you cannot prepare for the sleep deprivation. That helps to make the mental side of the race the toughest. You start an event on Monday and finish on Saturday. So you're going to be racing for five days non-stop – getting your head around that is hard. You're always nervous before a race, but as soon as you're an hour in it's OK. By the first night you think, 'Oh my god, we've been racing for 12 hours pretty hard, but we're only about 10 per cent into the race.' That can be daunting. As it goes on, you do get more into it and, before you know it, the first day is gone, then the second day, then you're halfway through: you really lose yourself in an adventure race.

You and your team are in a little bubble and you just disappear into a parallel universe and you just forget about everything. It's quite a bizarre sensation. It's a fantastic mental, physical and emotional journey. You have some high highs, but you will have lows – you're bound to be cold, tired, wet and hungry. The highs always outweigh the lows by a thousand times – it can be quite a rollercoaster of emotions.

You couldn't do the entire Adventure Race World Series in a year because your body would fall to pieces. But it is great. They're in fantastic locations. They're very well organised. It's a very friendly sport and there's really good camaraderie.

Nick Gracie was part of the team that won the 2009 Adventure Racing World Championships. He completes in multiple events around the world. For more information, visit teamadidasterrex.com

ATHLETE PERSPECTIVE

Type of event Underwater
Date All year
Distance of event Varies
Main obstacles Mental
Website www.aidainternational.com
They call it The ultimate way to free yourself and spend more time enjoying the beauty and silence of the sea.

Competitors say
❛ *Motivation comes from the exhilaration, the sense of being a pioneer and discovering something new about the human condition.* ❜

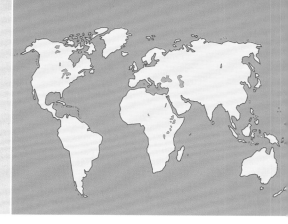

Freediving

An unencumbered journey into the deep blue sea. Freediving calls on supreme physical and mental strength as athletes reach depths and times that go way beyond what many deem physically possible.

opposite The key to freediving is complete relaxation

Freediving is anything. So much so that on one extreme it's probably possible to claim a legitimate freedive in a bath. On the other hand it is something different: it is focused; it is relaxed; and can be dangerous. At its core, freediving is the simple instance of holding your breath underwater.

As such, the origins of the sport go back as far as mankind itself. Scandinavian shell divers are known to have practised freediving as early as 5400 BC, and other instances around the Mediterranean and Egyptian coasts date back to similar periods. But it wasn't until 1949 that Raimondo Bucher took a 50,000 lire bet to dive down to 30m (98 feet) on a single breath hold, and freediving became a sport.

From those humble beginnings, the sport of freediving has metamorphosed into an international industry. Freediving – or apnoea diving – is taught in scuba schools around the world. Professional freedivers compete in events run by the sports governing bodies. These bodies record all historical achievements and oversee the execution of record-breaking attempts. Across the sport there are numerous categories, ranging from No Limit Dives, where competitors descend with the help of a ballast weight and ascend via a method of his or her choice, to Constant Weight with or without fins, where ascent and descent is through muscle strength alone.

With such differing disciplines the records and the achievements of the athletes are difficult to compare. For instance, in the No Limit category Herbert Nitsch achieved a world record dive of 214m (700 feet), which has yet to be beaten; Tanya Streeter holds the women's record at 160m (525 feet). However, in the Constant Weight without fins

category, William Trubridge holds the record at 101m (330 feet) – a mere 23m (75 feet) short of Herbert Nitsch's 124m (407 feet) world record with fins. Needless to say, achieving these sort of depths requires an exceptional ability to hold one's breath, and the record for Static Apnoea is 11 minutes, 35 seconds for men (set by Stephane Mifsud) and 8 minutes, 23 seconds for women (set by Natalia Molchanova).

As stand-alone records, these achievements in themselves are impressive. But it is the pressure that freediving puts on the body which makes the sport stand out as a supreme physical challenge. All mammals have what is known as the mammalian diving reflex. Strongest in mammals like dolphins, it is relatively primitive in the human body, and weakens as we get older. Triggered by cold water touching the face, the human body changes to facilitate survival at depth and with a lack of oxygen. These changes include a drop in heart rate, a contraction of blood vessels (keeping blood closer to the heart) and a reduction in the residual volume of the lungs so that when they compress to the size of a fist the chest cavity does not collapse.

But a freediver's ability to manage the body's reaction to the atmospheric pressure that they put themselves under is key to their success – and survival. Under the pressure of holding their breath for such extended periods of time, freedivers will experience diaphragmatic contractions as the body attempts to force respiration. These increase in frequency until nearly a constant, while mental faculties slowly begin to shut down and, eventually, the rapid onset of tunnel vision offers the last warning that the body is going into blackout.

As such, it can be a dangerous sport. When all of the

safety procedures are in place, competitors are relatively safe. However, things can go wrong, the most high profile fatality being that of record holder Audrey Mastre, who died during a 171m (560-foot) No Limits dive when the equipment on her diving sled failed. Freedivers never dive alone because of the danger of passing out at depth, and for those attempting record dives there are numerous support crew members to ensure both safety and the best possible opportunity for success.

But despite the dangers, freediving continues to attract supreme athletes to test themselves against both the ocean and their minds. Because unlike many sports, to achieve the greatest depths athletes must remain as calm as possible. Focus and relaxation are essential to enable the body and mind to cope with the pressure of going where few people can – or dare to – venture. But for those who do, the achievement is massive.

right The scenery is impressive, the challenge immense

Freediving is about the connection with the water. It is about pushing the body and mind to places that few dare to go – although many could if they tried. And unlike so many of the challenges in this book it is about releasing oneself from physical and mental pressure. A unique sport with quite spectacular rewards, freediving will push athletes way beyond their comfort zones in pursuit of the deep blue sea.

William Trubridge

Freediving is as much about mental preparation as it is about physical. I do a lot of training in the pool, the gym and yoga to increase my base and technique, working on my resistance to low oxygen and high carbon dioxide.

I do a lot to prepare myself mentally: meditation and visualisation. Breathing is definitely important. Just by concentrating on your breath you can slow everything down – your thoughts and your body's patterns. But ultimately mental preparedness comes from a deep state of just being comfortable with what you are doing, with your preparation and knowing that you have the dive in you. All of this allows you to be in a state when you are not anxious about the dive, because if that happens your heart rate goes up and you use more oxygen.

In a deep freedive you don't really look around you or observe much. If you did, then you would use much more oxygen. I guess it's the difference between going into a museum and looking at all the exhibits or just sitting in a dark room. One is a lot more exhausting than the other. When freediving, you want to go inside yourself and shut down all the stimuli and the mental processes so you can conserve oxygen for just getting down there and back.

It probably sounds a bit boring, but at the same time it can be quite liberating and a beautiful experience because you feel like you've gone inside yourself for those few minutes. It's very dark and completely quiet. There's very little light stimuli and no sound stimuli. Touch is pretty much uniform everywhere. You can't feel gravity or your own weight very much. So to a certain extent you're outside your own body because all of the senses are very passive and not receiving anything.

The sport isn't as dangerous as it is made out to be. You have safety divers there who are trained and experienced. If something goes wrong or you run out of breath, it's most likely to happen right at the end of the dive when you are close to the surface or in most cases after you've surfaced and you've taken your first breath – that's when a blackout occurs. Obviously, if you are by yourself and a blackout occurs, then the outcome can be different.

I'm motivated by the exhilaration, the sense of being a pioneer and discovering something new about the human condition. It is that sense of discovery. That's the existential motive. But the more basic motivation is how beautiful an experience it is to hold your breath and be part of that underwater realm which is so incredibly different to how we live our lives above the surface.

In 2010 William Trubridge became the first person in history to freedive to 100m (330 feet) without any assistance of any kind. For more information, on William, visit verticalblue.net

Type Sailing | **Date** Varies
Distance 39,396km (24,480 miles)
Main obstacles Weather, mental, distance,
    conditions, technical
Website www.vendeeglobe.org/en
They call it A sailing race around the world,
    for single-handers, without any stopovers.
    That's it. In theory at least …

Competitors say
❛The ultimate personal challenge of you and your boat, using nature to complete a lap of the planet unassisted.❜

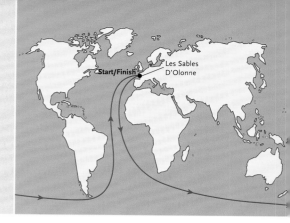

Start/Finish — Les Sables D'Olonne

Vendée Globe

It is a voyage into the unknown. A complete circumnavigation of the globe with no stopping points, no assistance, and nowhere to hide from the ferocious wind and waves that batter parts of the Southern Hemisphere. The toughest sailing race on Earth? Yes. The toughest race on Earth? Quite possibly.

below Human and boat against the elements

In 1989 Frenchman Philippe Jeantot decided to change sailing forever. Having won the BOC Challenge (now called the 5 Oceans Race), he wanted to go further. He wanted to organise a race that pushed those who dared to tackle it to the very limit. 'Time,' he wrote, 'is a necessary factor to attain perfect harmony with one's sailboat. A round-the-world race, without stopovers or assistance, such were the conditions to reach the desired communion.'

Thirteen sailors joined him on the startline of the inaugural Vendée Globe. None of them had ever spent more than 100 days alone at sea before. Six of the 13 did not finish the race. Frenchman Titouan Lamazou took the win in 109 days, 8 hours and 48 minutes. Jeantot was fourth (113 days, 23 hours and 47 minutes) and Jean-Francois Coste was the final competitor across the line (163 days, 1 hour, 19 minutes). A legendary race was born.

The Vendée Globe is unique in that there is an approximate course, but it is by no means set in stone. The simple objective laid out for competitors is that they 'must sail around the world without either stopovers or any external "help"'. And of course, there are ways and means of doing this: tackling the Northwest or Northeast Passage (which is short of the 33,796km/21,000 miles required distance and usually ice-bound); or by heading south from the start/finish point in Les Sables D'Olonne and rounding both the Cape of Good Hope and Cape Horn. A route via the Panama and Suez Canals requires outside assistance and so is prohibited.

above The start
before the solitude

So the race heads south, before turning 'left' once the boats hit the Southern Ocean. This way, the route is clear and the sailor can benefit from the prevailing westerly winds. This also allows competitors to pass through the eight gates laid out on the course and so complete the race proper.

But going south is not without its challenges. Extremes of temperature and weather greet sailors throughout the race, but once they round the Cape of Good Hope they enter an area of the ocean known in nautical circles as the Roaring Forties and the Furious Fifties. With little land mass stopping the winds from whipping across the ocean, sailors benefit from the prevailing winds, but they are also at their mercy. Churning seas with swells in excess of 30m (98 feet) greet competitors, propelling the boats forward at often startling speeds.

These ferocious seas are tackled alone by competitors, and that is surely the toughest aspect of the Vendée Globe. Competitors have some contact with the outside world

through satellite phones and radio, but help is limited. They also have plenty of information on the position of the competition, adding to the intensity of the race environment. But while they are allowed to anchor en route, they cannot stop at a port. So as they head into the Southern Ocean they truly are alone. As such, if anything goes wrong with their boats, if they have any physical problems, or if they capsize they have to be entirely self-sufficient until help can arrive – and that could easily take hours or days.

That is why all competitors are required to take medical and survival courses. They must also have completed a qualifying race on the same boat that they intend to use for the Vendée. Under Vendée rules, this is an 18m (60-foot)

IMOCA. For over three months, this boat is their living, eating, sleeping but most importantly working quarters. Specially designed to tackle the unique challenges facing competitors, the design of the boats is relatively flexible – although there are strict safety measures in place to ensure the optimum opportunity for competitor survival.

And most do survive. In every race there are casualties, and competitors are frequently forced to withdraw with broken boats or bones. In fact, of the 30 starters in the 2008/9 race, 19 failed to finish. But while the percentage of DNFs may have risen, the time it takes to complete the race has dropped. From 109 days in 1989 to just 84 days, 3 hours and 9 minutes in 2008/9– Michel Desjoyeaux finished more than three weeks ahead of his 'rivals' from 20-years previously.

Of all the races that feature in this book, few are truly solo efforts. The Vendée Globe is. An adventure into the unknown, facing up to challenges that for many of us are imperceptible. Not least, the challenge of being completely alone, with no land or help for thousands of miles around. The Vendée Globe is a true test of human endurance, and one that captures the imaginations of sailors – and the general public – every time it takes place.

left The joy of finishing

Dee Caffari

I came to the Vendée Globe after an opportunity set up by Sir Chay Blythe to tackle what was considered going the 'wrong' way around the world. (The other way: down the bottom, turn right.) For me to be the first woman to do this was quite unique, but I was very aware as I crashed through the Southern Ocean that everybody else goes the other way. So I decided that I wanted to find out why they go that way, and it seemed much easier in comparison. And if you're going to put yourself out there to do that, then the ultimate way to do it is with the best sailors in the world in the pinnacle event, which is the Vendée Globe.

Preparing for a race like this is tough. Everybody thinks that the biggest thing would be the sailing and how to sail a boat fast, but it's all the peripheral things that are often underrated – like the psychological preparation, the weather training, tactical awareness of the strategy when you're out there racing, as well as preparing the boat and for all the 'what if' scenarios if things go wrong.

This race is more about learning how to manage yourself, being aware of the eating, drinking and sleeping so that you can make sure you aren't emotionally drained and can concentrate your efforts into performance – getting to the end. It isn't a short race – it's intense for a long period of time.

When you're out on the boat, you get a position report and so you know exactly where everybody else is and how fast they are going. That really does intensify the competition. You're out there doing your own thing, but you know where everybody else is – it is ultimately a race. So it's about pushing on the edge so that you don't push too far and break it, but it's also about getting to the

end of it. In that respect it's about understanding your boat and personal limitations so that you can cross the finish line.

The 2008/9 Vendée Globe is the perfect example where 30 boats started and 11 crossed the finish line.

Of course, there's a certain element of Lady Luck when you're dealing with nature. You don't have any control over what the weather is going to deal you – that's for sure. But getting to the end is about tenacity and digging deep and getting through the worst bits so that you can push on the good bits, where the benefits will be much greater. Once you have an understanding of the time to push and the time to hold back, you get to enjoy it as well. But you do need to find some deep resources; tenacity and mental toughness are the attributes that get you to the end.

Sailing the Southern Ocean is everything it's reputed to be and more; it's a real double-edged sword. The magic, the wonder, the solitude, the hostile environment, the wonderful albatrosses, the severe storms, the risk of icebergs or imminent danger; it's this whole adrenaline rush rolled into one. You have this emotional rollercoaster of enjoying the good bits, being terrified by the bad bits and surviving through it. There's a certain magic about being down there in a place where not many people get to go, where rescue isn't around apart from your fellow competitors, that attracts us all and makes us want to go back.

In 2006 Dee Caffari became the first woman to sail the 'wrong way' around the planet. She came sixth in the 2008/9 Vendée Globe.

Index

Acknowledgements

Thanks to all who supplied photography for this book:

24-Hour Track Race © Paul Moore, pages 128, 129; courtesy of the Ottawa 24hr Race, page 130 (all three) ■ **4 Deserts** © www.racingtheplanet.com, pages 185–189 (all) ■ **6633 Extreme Winter Ultra Marathon** © Martin Like/6633, pages 8 (bottom left), 151–153 (all) ■ **Adventure Racing World Series** © Gareth Dyer, page 194; James Pitman, pages 195, 196; Owen Hughes, page 197 ■ **Al Andalus Ultimate Trail Race** © James Goldsmith, pages 9 (top left), 23–26 (all) ■ **Arrowhead 135** © Arrowhead 135, pages 106–107 (all) ■ **Badwater Ultramarathon** © Ahren Trumble, pages 8–9 (bottom), 142–145 (all) ■ **Cadiz Freedom Swim** © Janet McCallum, pages 64, 65 (top); Rodger Bosch, pages 65 (bottom), 66; Marc Wessels, page 67 ■ **Cape Epic** © Sven Martin/Cape Epic, page 68; Gary Perkin/Cape Epic, pages 69, 70 ■ **Catalina Channel Swim** © Paula Selby, pages 115–117 (all) ■ **Coast to Coast New Zealand** © Paul's Camera Shop Christchurch, pages 101–102 (all) ■ **Comrades Marathon** © Comrades Marathon, pages 75–77 (all) ■ **Crocodile Trophy** © Regina Stanger, pages 1, 98–100 (all) ■ **Devizes to Westminster International Canoe Race** © Susie Brown, page 37; Chris Wingham, page 38; Paul Andrews, page 39 ■ **Dusi Canoe Marathon** © Gameplan Media, pages 78–80 (all) ■ **Enduroman Arch to Arc** © RAF/Crown Copyright, pages 34–36 (all) ■ **English Channel Swim** © Bryony Taylor Edwards, page 41; Eva Asderaki, page 42; Bryony Taylor Edwards, page 43 ■ **The Extreme World Races South Pole Race** © www.extremeworldraces.com, pages 5, 176–179 (all) ■ **Freediving** © Sergey Orlov, pages 8 (middle), 199, 200–201 ■ **Furnace Creek 508** © Ben Jones, pages 146–148 (all) ■ **Great Wall Marathon** © www.adventure-marathon.com, pages 88–90 (all) ■ **Iditarod** © Matt Cooper, page 131; Louise Cukrov, pages 132–133 ■ **Iron Bike** © Cable Press/Daniel Julian, pages 47, 48 ■ **Jungle Marathon** © Gil Serique/Jungle Marathon, pages 167–170 (all) ■ **Kalahari Augrabies Extreme Marathon** © Sandy Wild, pages 4, 62, 63; Jessica Walker, pages 60–61; Joan Kreim, page 61 ■ **La Haute Route** © Manu Molle/La Haute Route, pages 30–33 (all) ■ **La Ruta de Los Conquistadores** © J. Andrés Vargas/Lead Adventure Media, pages 171–173 (all) ■ **Leadville 100** © Glen Delman, pages 109–111 (all) ■ **Manhattan Island Marathon Swim** © Vladimir Brezina, pages 122, 123 (both) ■ **Marathon Des Sables** © CIMBALY-RASTOIN-MDS2011, pages 6–7, 82–83; CIMBALY-PERMDS2011, pages 83, 84, 85 ■ **The Mountainman** © BergArena, pages 1–2 (main), 51–53 (all) ■ **Norseman** © Kai-Otto Melau/NXTRI, pages 12–14 (all) ■ **Ö till Ö** © Malcolm Hanes/Ö till Ö 2011, pages 27–29 (all) ■ **Patagonian Expedition Race** © Luis Bertea, page 9 (right); Walter Alvial, pages 162, 163, 165; Valentino Saldivar, page 164 ■ **Race Across America** © Chris Milliman, pages 118, 119, 120 (bottom); Jeff Orlowski, page 120 (top); Rick Boethling, page 121 ■ **Race Around Ireland** © LUPI SPUMA, pages 44–45 (both)

■ **Red Bull X-Alps** © Felix Woelk/Red Bull Content Pool, page 16; Vitek Ludvik/Red Bull Content Pool, pages 17 (top right and main), 18 ■ **Self Transcendence 3100 Mile Race** © Jowan Gauthier, pages 157–158 (all) ■ **Spartathlon** © Spartathlon, pages 55–57 (all) ■ **Tevis Cup Ride** © courtesy of The Tevis Cup, pages 125, 126 (both) ■ **Tour d'Afrique** © Philip Hart, page 71; Chris Evans, page 72 (left); Joachim Loeffel, pages 72–73 (middle); Kelsey Wiens, page 74 ■ **Trans Europe Footrace** © Ingo Schulze/Transeurope Footrace, pages 20–21 (all) ■ **Ultraman World Championships** © Josh Baker/Enduro Photo, pages 154, 155 (both) ■ **Vendée Globe** © Jacques Vapillon/vapillon. com, pages 202–205 ■ **Volvo Ocean Race** © Ainhoa Sanchez, page 190; Ian Roamn, page 191; Nico Martinez, page 192 (top left); Sander van der Borch, page 192 (bottom right) ■ **Western States 100** © Joe McCladdie, pages 112–113 (all) ■ **Woodvale Challenge** © Ben Thackwray, pages 182–184 (all) ■ **Yak Attack** © Phil Stasiw, pages 91–95 (all) ■ **Yukon Arctic Ultra** © Dave Berridge, page 135; Yann Besrest-Butler, page 136; Mark Gillett, page 137 ■ **Yukon Quest** © Harry Kern Photography, pages 139–141 (all).

This book would not have been possible without the help of a number of people who we frequently asked to go above and beyond the call of duty. In no particular order:

Nadia Arndt, Michelle Cutler, Dave Pramann, Chris Kostman, Forrest Nelson, Ahren Trumble, Datuk Balawant Singh Kler, Pete Clayden, Tom Purvis, Tom Armistead, Ray de Vries, Brett Austen Smith, Megan Hall, Julie Royer, Erica Dao, Karen Jayne Leinberger, Hannah Borgeson, Andy Weinberg, Florian Spichtig, Michael Lemmel, Darika Joyce Friesen, Utsahi St.-Amand, Rick Boethling, Alan Heary, Theresa Brown, Henry Gold, Ingo Schulze, Jane Bockus, Christina Gaither, John Trent, Joe McCladdie, Nadeem Khan, Tarquin Cooper, Dave Berridge, Robert Pollhammer, Martin Like, Tanya Odendaal, Thami Vilakazi, Sue Thomas, Regina Stanger, Jean-Charles Lievens, Frances Chan, Joanna Moyser, William Trubridge, Martin Nobbs, Pixie Ingram, Ben Thackwray, Eva Asderaki, Christian Roemhild, Rachael Cadman, Dan Crofton, Kevin Russ, Phil Evans, Kate Riordan, Genevieve Stroombergen, Gerhard Schoenbacher, Farah Manuel, Shirley Thompson, Gitte Sorensen, Craig Bycroft, Ryan Sandes, Nick Gracie, Anna Scott, Tony Martin and, from Bloomsbury, Charlotte Atyeo, Charlotte Croft and Nick Ascroft. If there is anyone we have missed out we apologise profusely and thank you sincerely.

Finally, we would like to thank our families and friends for their unwavering support and encouragement throughout this process.